Cybersecurity Essentials: A No-Nonsense Guide for SMBs

By David Henderson

© 2021 David Henderson.

All rights reserved. This book or any portion thereof may not be reproduced or used in any manner whatsoever without the publisher's express written permission except for the use of brief quotations in a book review or scholarly journal.

First Printing: 2021

ISBN 978-1-7947-2959-9

Published by
MSP Author
Computer Center, Inc. 39 S Main St
Ste. 300
Janesville, WI 53545
www.mspbookauthor.com
Helping MSPs Become Authors

This publication is designed to provide accurate and authoritative information regarding the subject matter covered. It is sold with the understanding that the publisher is not engaged in rendering legal, accounting, or other professional advice. If legal advice or other expert assistance is required, the services of a competent professional should be sought.

This title is available at special quantity discounts for bulk purchase for sales promotions, premiums, fundraising, and educational use.

For more information, please contact
David Henderson
CyberStreams
951 Industry Drive
Tukwila, WA 98188
www.cyberstreams.com
(206)737-0841

TABLE OF CONTENTS

SECTION I: RANSOMWARE: THE GREATEST THREAT TO YOUR SMALL BUSINESS 1
- INTRODUCTION 3
- ARE THE BAD GUYS REALLY AFTER MY BUSINESS? 7
- WHAT IS A DATA BREACH? 9
- WHAT IS RANSOMWARE? 13
- HOW IS RANSOMWARE DELIVERED? 15
- THE DARK WEB THREAT 19
- HOW ARE YOUR CREDENTIALS EXPOSED? 21
- WHAT ARE STOLEN CREDENTIALS USED FOR? 23
- HUMANS: THE TARGETS AND THE DEFENSE 25

SECTION II: PROTECTING YOUR SMALL BUSINESS 27
- RATING YOUR COMPANY'S TECHNOLOGICAL MATURITY 29
- DEFENSE IN DEPTH 31
- AWARENESS: YOUR SMALL BUSINESS DEFENSE 35
- CREATING A CYBERSECURITY CULTURE 37
- MULTI-FACTOR AUTHENTICATION: YOUR NEW BEST FRIEND 41
- CYBER RESILIENCE 43
- SIX CYBERSECURITY TIPS ANY SMALL BUSINESS CAN IMPLEMENT 45
- 7 COST-EFFECTIVE ADVANCED SECURITY STEPS 47
- ZERO TRUST 51
- HOW MANY BERRIES DO YOU HAVE STORED UP? 55
- DOING BUSINESS WITH THE DOD 57

SECTION III: THE SMALL BUSINESS GUIDE TO CYBERSECURITY IMPLEMENTATION 61
- NINE MINIMAL STEPS TO BETTER PROTECTION 63
- THE 7 ESSENTIAL LAYERS OF SECURITY 69
- ZERO TRUST FOR YOUR SMALL BUSINESS 77
- ASSEMBLING YOUR INCIDENCE RESPONSE TEAM 81
- SAMPLE SECURITY INCIDENT RESPONSE 85
- SAMPLE BREACH RESPONSE LETTER 91
- WHAT SHOULD YOU DO IF YOU GET RANSOMED? 93
- PULLING IT ALL TOGETHER 97
- GLOSSARY 99

RESOURCES 105

About the Author

Dave Henderson has more than 30 years of experience in IT.

He has a rich set of skills from software design to executive leadership. David's passion for IT started at Fairview Middle school in 1981 when he learned how to program BASIC on a Prime mainframe computer. David's career includes CRM and software development. Before co-founding CyberStreams, an outsourced IT company supporting small businesses and non-profits in the Seattle and Austin areas, he worked as a website developer.

David holds a certificate in Software Development Design from the University of Washington. In addition, David has been a panelist and guest speaker at dozens of private and public events. He is especially proud to have shared the stage with FBI and FAA cyberespionage agents at the Pacific Northwest Aerospace Alliance annual conference.

David is happily married to his high school sweetheart, Lisa. Their daughter is just starting her career as a defense attorney, and their son specializes in microbiology laboratory testing. Lisa and David live in their hometown of Bremerton, a ferry ride away from Seattle.

https://www.cyberstreams.com/

Section I: Ransomware:
The Greatest Threat to Your Small Business

Introduction

You know, running a small business is hard enough these days. The past two years certainly haven't made your job as a business owner and entrepreneur any less stressful.

Due to COVID-19, the world has become even more dependent on technology and forced to react to the threat by quickly sending staff home.

We've seen increased cyberattacks against small businesses more than ever, just like yours. Unfortunately, while business owners like you struggle to keep their businesses afloat, cybercriminals have seized this opportunity to ramp up attacks on companies like yours.

Does the thought of having your data wiped out, your computer system rendered useless, and the horrible, sinking feeling of knowing that you're being held hostage by some scumbag trying to make a buck at your expense keep you up at night? Well, it does me!

Small companies are especially vulnerable to cyberattacks of this nature. In 2018, small companies were the target in 71% of cyber assaults, with an average demand of $116,000. Small businesses, who are less likely to have a backup of their data, are more likely to pay the ransom, and they must act immediately (Rosenbaum, 2021). It's really due to a lack of planning and know-how.

The news is filled with reports of attacks against big companies and organizations, medical facilities, and governments. The massive dollar amounts involved in ransomware cases such as these sell papers.

But smaller companies, like yours and mine, are at risk too.

Significant data breaches, like the JBS Meat Packing plant breach in 2021 or the Colonial Pipeline breach, fill the headlines. However, it's small companies that should be most concerned. In contrast, the following examples of ransomware attacks against small businesses illustrate how even one cyberattack can cripple a small business like yours.

Take, for example, Main Construction, a small business that lost $588,000 to a cyberattack when the bad guys acquired bank accounts and made a series of ACH transactions. Although the bank retrieved some of the funds, Main Construction still lost $345,445.00! (Weaver, 2021)

Hackers targeted Green Ford Sales, a car dealership. In under 24 hours, the hackers had added nine fake employees to the company's payroll and paid them $63,000.00. Green Ford could only cancel a portion of the transactions, resulting in a $23,000.00 loss.

Volunteer Voyages lost more than $14,000 due to a stolen bank card. When the owner returned from a trip to Peru, he was shocked to discover that his account was hacked, a corporate card number stolen, and the account closed. Although he alerted the bank of his overseas travel, the bank refused to pay him.

These cases emphasize that small company owners will not be compensated if their accounts are hacked (Freitas, 2021). Even though a single individual owns the Voyages Volunteers, the bank stated that it was under no duty to refund the owner.

I know you're great at running your business and serving your customers. Chances are, you're like one of the two types of business owners that I meet. Which group are you in?

One group doesn't value their technology and may even believe that they aren't a target for any cyberattack or crippling ransomware attack. When I talk to business owners like this, they are convinced that what they have in place is good enough. They don't value their technology but see it as a commodity. Of course, that only lasts until they have a cyberattack event. Then it's a different story. I hope that you're not one of those folks.

If you are, then this book is for you. I hope that by the end of this book, you'll at least have a better appreciation of just how real this threat is.

The next group of business owners I encounter is those that see their technology strategically. It's not just a commodity like an office chair or desk. It's a tool that can improve efficiency and help them compete. They realize that technology is an investment in their business, not an expense.

These clients tell me repeatedly how the possibility of getting ransomware or having one of their employees click on a phishing email and expose their company to a data breach scares them to death. I hope you fall more into this second category. However, suppose you are still leaning in the other direction. In that case, I sincerely hope that you'll have at least a healthy fear or concern about how serious ransomware and cybersecurity are by the end of this book.

This book is also for you because I will give you some concrete steps to make your network even more secure.

Even minor breaches can cost thousands of dollars not only in actual ransom money but in downtime, loss of clients, IT costs, and even loss of reputation.

That kind of stuff scares the heck out of me and should scare you too.

Now, I'm not here to just scare you. I also want to give you some solutions. So we're going to talk about specific ways you can protect your small business, regardless of the size, even if you don't have an IT department or work with an outside consultant.

I'm going to include things you can do yourself or have a one-time price tag, meaning you can start implementing this protection after you've finished this book.

Of course, if you have any questions or would like to discuss how Cyberstreams can help you implement any of these solutions, I'd be happy to have a one-on-one conversation.

So, let's get started and dive into protecting your business from the bad guys.

Are the Bad Guys REALLY after MY Business?

One of the most frequent questions I get when talking about cybersecurity threats is, "Are they really after me and my business?" Most small business owners and entrepreneurs I speak to ask me this. They explain that they can't possibly have anything of value to hackers that would make them a target.

Honestly, I wish this were true. And I can understand why so many small businesses falsely believe this. After all even though, the news is full of ransomware attacks, the focus is on large organizations, not small companies like ours. But, the media loves to report on sensational stories of multi-million dollar ransoms affecting giant corporations.

Unfortunately, statistics tell us otherwise. Current estimates state that 1 in 4 small businesses fall victim to some sort of data breach or cybersecurity attack. Further, even though the news is filled with multi-million-dollar ransomware stories, the average ransom for a small business is $4,300.00. Now, I don't know about you, but that's not chump change for my small business.

What you need to understand is that cyberattacks are predominately automated. This means that threat actors are casting a vast net. They are harvesting our credentials, such as emails and other personal information, from the dark web using automated software to send out millions of phishing emails, hoping to snare a few prospects who then, in turn, they can begin to focus on.

This automation allows them to attack businesses of all sizes, including yours, indiscriminately.

Furthermore, the IT industry believes that the statistics are much higher, approaching 50%. It's just that most small businesses don't report the data breach, despite any regulations, for fear of losing clients or tarnishing their reputations.

You also need to know that the bad guys are organized and professional, and for them, this is a full-time job.

Take this interview with a cybercriminal, for example: "*How would you define yourself with respect to the hacking activities you are conducting? I*'m a Black Hat. This means that hacking is my job and gives me salary. I run black-ops for those hiring me. I'm quite expensive." (Cisco)

Ransomware is big business. Yes, ransomware is an organized business. The recent Colonial Pipeline and JBS Meat plant attacks exemplify how devastating ransomware can be.

We've all gotten the spam telephone call about our expired car warranty. In the background, you hear the sounds of a call center. That is exactly what is happening.

The media finally talks about organized hackers such as Anonymous and DarkSide (responsible for the Colonial Pipeline ransomware attack). However, we've also seen increased cyberespionage attacks against US-based governments and businesses. This was evident in the Hafnium attacks, which targeted small businesses with in-house Microsoft Exchange servers. Even small companies with a few employees who had internal networks with Microsoft servers were affected.

The American Bar Association (ABA) estimates that 30% of small law firms still have Exchange servers in their offices because they believe, falsely, that this approach was more secure than moving to the cloud. Unfortunately, this incident proved that to be incorrect.

In short, regardless of the size or industry of your small business, whether you have 1 or 100 employees, you (as are all of us) are at risk of a ransomware attack or other data breach. These breaches can cripple your business for days if you are not prepared and cost thousands of dollars, not only in ransom costs but also in the expense of restoring data and rebuilding your network.

What Is a Data Breach?

Before we begin our discussion on ransomware and the dark web, we need to define what exactly a data breach is.

The official definition of a data breach is the "intentional or unintentional release of secure, private, or confidential information."

I want to break this definition down into its separate components, and then we will come back to how this relates to the rising ransomware and dark web threats.

First, think about all the data you store on your computer systems, network, cloud software, email, and even your mobile devices like tablets and phones. Chances are very high that you can quickly and easily identify private data. Things you would not release into the world like credit card or banking information and passwords to important websites. Perhaps your old tax returns or company financials are stashed away in a folder.

Next, consider all the data you store about your clients that they might not want to be exposed to the world. Of course, the above examples apply here as well. We also hear about medical records and health information, both private and protected information.

If you're in a regulated industry such as the health care, financial, or legal industries, you may have additional regulations governing what data can and cannot be shared publicly. For example, lawyers may not even be allowed to release who they represent.

The fact that you provide counseling or mental health services to a client also falls into that category of protected information.

So now we have an idea of the types of data you store and what should be considered private and confidential.

It's also important to consider this when you have a breach because different laws govern the actions you are required to take if a data breach occurs.

The general data breach laws in Washington require businesses to disclose a breach. In addition, the law defines the following items as personal information: name, social security number, financial account numbers, passwords, account numbers, DNA, and just about anything not already publicly available.

(https://app.leg.wa.gov/RCW/default.aspx?cite=19.255.010)

This is a fairly broad definition because it applies to nearly everyone in business in our state and almost any data we hold for our clients.

Okay, now that we've established that we all have a legal obligation to protect our clients' data and report it if it is obtained by anyone else, let's look at what that means in terms of ransomware and the dark web.

In both situations, the attackers (or threat actors, as everyone seems to like to call them these days) obtain your data. Later on, we'll go into greater detail about how this happens and how to defend yourself. But for now, know that if you suffer a ransomware attack or any of your credentials for various accounts you use are exposed on the dark web, you may be required to report it as a data breach.

Before going any further, please step back and consider the seriousness of that. What if you had to report to all your clients, past and present, that their data, with which you were entrusted, had been stolen and potentially exposed? What would the business and reputational damage be like? What would it cost you to notify all those people?

As we will see, the goal of ransomware is to leverage your data and your client's data to hold your company for ransom or extort money from you with the threat of exposing it to others.

Many small businesses, especially those not in a regulated industry like the ones I mention above, feel that they are too small to worry about such a breach even happening in the first place. Unfortunately, that's simply not the case.

While the news loves to report on tremendous, sensational stories like the Colonial Pipeline and JBS Meat plant breaches, estimates are that at least 25-35% of all small businesses experience a breach. In my industry, we believe that number is even higher, but, despite the laws, small businesses don't report the breach for fear and embarrassment.

Here are a few examples of how your data can be breached or exposed to the outside world.

- Malware infections and cyberattacks on un or under-protected systems. This includes both ransomware and other viruses.

- Not using technology correctly. User error is a big part of data breaches, as we will discuss at length. Even if your IT department or provider has put technological safeguards in place, individuals can still allow threat actors and malware into your business through improper use of the technology. For example, if an email filter requires a specific action on the sender's part to encrypt

and protect a message, but the sender fails to take that action, despite the technology being in place.
- A client is communicating insecurely. Sometimes, the clients you serve are releasing the information as they communicate with you. Therefore, you need to discuss the proper ways to communicate with your company and educate your clients on using secure technology.
- Human error and mistakes. We all make mistakes, so sending off an email with sensitive data before it's encrypted is something we all might do. Losing a laptop or portable device or even falling for a phishing scam are simple mistakes that we all can make.
- A worker may intentionally expose data. Usually, this is done maliciously, such as by a disgruntled employee.

To summarize, a data breach is the release of personal or protected data to an outside source, regardless of how that data was exposed.

What is Ransomware?

I'll assume that you are at least somewhat familiar with computer viruses. They've been around since the early years of computing. In the "good old days," these viruses were primarily benign, sometimes displaying a silly screen or message and, at worse, destroying some data. But, in many ways, these were simply curious kids pushing the boundaries of new technology and proving to each other what they could do.

The Internet, however, allows malicious software to report back to the creators, making malware a dangerous two-way street. This means that if a piece of malware infects your computer, it can 'phone home' and let the authors know that it now has access to your computer. It may then be able to send information back to them, record your keystrokes, send files, even take screenshots, or use the camera on your computer.

Ransomware is malicious software (like a virus) that infects a computer and quietly scrambles your data (encrypting it), making it inaccessible. It enters your computer or network like any other malware by tricking users into clicking links to download it or by infecting websites you visit (including legitimate websites where ads can carry this malicious software).

Once installed on your computer, ransomware begins to scramble your data quietly. Once encrypted, the ransomware presents you with a popup message demanding payment for a key to unlock the data.

Payment is usually demanded in Bitcoin and can range from a few hundred to a few thousand dollars for a small business. (CIS)

The attackers even provide phone numbers and technical support to assist you in making your payments and retrieving your data, hoping that you will pay the ransom in exchange for a key to unlocking your data. That is the business model.

Recently, criminals have taken this to a new level to increase the likelihood that you will pay the ransom. Ransoms typically increase in price the longer you wait, expecting you to react quickly and pay the ransom instead of looking for alternatives such as hiring an IT company to assist or restoring a backup.

Additional tactics now include two forms of extortion. In the first case, the ransomware creators threaten to publicly expose all you and your customers' data if you don't pay up. The obvious intent here is, once again, to make sure you pay instead of simply restoring your data and moving on.

The third approach is to begin holding your clients' ransom as well. Imagine that you are breached, and the data includes private and confidential information about your clients. This data can be account information, social security numbers, or medical or legal information. Since the data kidnappers have access to all this data, usually including names, phone numbers, and email addresses, they now turn to your clients and threaten to release their information publicly unless they pay a ransom.

Your reputation is threatened, and your clients may learn about the data breach, whether you intended for them to find out or not.

Cybercriminals are getting more sophisticated in their tactics to infiltrate our businesses and the means and methods they use to extract a ransom from you. If this doesn't scare you, even a little bit, I don't know what will.

How is Ransomware Delivered?

In 2020 we faced significant, rapid changes in how and where we work due to COVID-19. Suddenly we found our employees working from home. This change happened very quickly and, much to the chagrin of the IT industry, often with very few security policies and procedures in place. This shift caused a surge in ransomware as a means of accessing our personal and business data.

Attacks rose by more than 150% over the previous year, and the amount paid to hackers increased by more than 300%. (Harvard Business Review) Much of this was due to people using unsecured computers on home networks. These fell outside the standard control and management of IT departments. In addition, there was very little thought about security for small businesses, so the minimal security found in even the least sophisticated small businesses, such as a basic firewall and a computer dedicated only to business work, didn't even exist.

Further, attackers took advantage of this shift nearly immediately. Increased reliance on email as the primary form of communication, even amongst people in the same office, allows for more phishing attacks.

Businesses suddenly had to learn new technologies like video conferencing solutions such as Zoom, which was plagued by cyberattacks.

Ransomware is growing in sophistication, as are how threat actors deliver these attacks.

Of course, the primary goal is to find a way to circumvent whatever technological security you have in place. This is accomplished by targeting individuals or other known vulnerabilities. (Hisox)

Here are some shocking statistics:
- 65% of companies attacked reported it was due to phishing. This number grew to 74% in businesses with ten or fewer employees.
- 43% come from credential theft, reuse of passwords.
- 30% come from unpatched computers.

Unpatched computers remain a primary target for hackers. Most smaller businesses rely on automatic updaters for this. However, these are prone to failure and require a computer system's interaction (such as a reboot) to complete. Unfortunately, automatic updates for Windows or third-party software such as Adobe products, web browsers, and teleconferencing software can fail without warning or obvious notification to the user.

On more occasions than I can count, I've reviewed a prospect's network and found that they are months behind despite their complete assurance that all their computers are up-to-date with the latest software and security patches.

Of course, no amount of hardware or software protection can ever be 100% effective against any threat. The bad guys are working hard to find vulnerabilities that have yet to be remedied and change their tactics to keep us on our toes. Even high-level cybersecurity experts admit to being fooled at times. It's no wonder that those of us busy trying to run our businesses without cybersecurity degrees can easily fall prey to the latest techniques.

I'll also emphasize what I said before: cybercrime is a business for many people, and it's a full-time job that they take seriously. So with someone working that diligently to access your information, it's no wonder we get fooled.

Email continues to be one of the best delivery methods for phishing scams that look to trick users into clicking on links, installing unwanted software, or disclosing credentials that can be used to deliver ransomware in other ways. It used to be that you could easily spot a phishing scam by its poor grammar and spelling errors. However, this is less the case now.

There are numerous examples of emails being written near perfectly, even matching the tone and voice of the supposed sender, who the victim may know. Further, fake websites look so close to the originals that it's nearly impossible to tell them apart from legitimate ones.

Threat actors are also opportunistic. During COVID, successful phishing attacks revolved around those that mentioned COVID topics. These appear to be from legitimate sources asking the recipient to schedule vaccinations or find out more information about the virus.

Finally, ransomware and associated phishing scams are now a turnkey business opportunity on the dark web. Much like buying a series of legal templates or templates for documents or a presentation you're about to give, you can go online and purchase a complete package and start your own ransomware business in hours without even writing the software.

One such package I recently encountered included everything you need to do so. It was pre-made software that you could customize with the included application, a decryption key, and even an email series.

A few other ways that ransomware is delivered:
- Malvertising. Ads on legitimate sites that deliver malware.
- Using your existing credentials.
- Software vulnerabilities.

As users, we are indeed the weakest link in the security chain. Ultimately, education and training protect you and your data from thieves. Unfortunately, no amount of software or hardware security is 100% effective and, if staff aren't knowledgeable about how those protections work, they can easily still allow infections into your network by falling for the growingly sophisticated techniques that cybercriminals are using.

The Dark Web Threat

You may have heard the term "dark web" before, but I've found that few people truly understand it or brush it off as something that exists only in the movies.

When I find someone who at least understands the dark web, they usually fail to grasp the threat it poses and how it's related to ransomware and identity theft.

I'm here to tell you that the dark web is a real place and probably one of the scariest threats we face today.

I like to explain the dark web like this:

Before the Internet, organized or not, criminals would meet in dark alleys, seedy bars, and secret locations to trade goods and information. This may have included credit cards, stolen property, or even drugs and weapons.

Of course, these places still exist today, in the physical world.

The dark web is the Internet equivalent of these dark alleys. It comprises websites, storefronts, forums, and chat rooms where our information, such as our credit cards, accounts and passwords, social security numbers, and identities, are bought, sold, and traded.

These dark corners of the Internet are not places that you can search for or hop in and visit. Like the criminal underworld in the physical world, these require knowing the right people, the correct password, and the connections.

However, once you're in, you'll find eBay-like auction sites where you can bid on information databases.

You'll also find turnkey business opportunities!

Complete ransomware packages are sold here as well. Want to run a ransomware campaign? You can purchase a business-in-a-box for just a few hundred dollars. It includes pre-written and customizable ransomware software. You don't even need to write a computer program because many packages have customization tools that you just launch and run.

Your new ransomware business will also include instructions and tutorials, landing pages, and phishing emails ready for you to use, just as if you were buying a franchise!

Hop on over to another forum, and you can pick yourself up millions of known good emails, passwords, names, and other personal information to get you started right away.

The dark web and ransomware are linked. They thrive together in these communities of criminals. And that's where your credentials and data are bought and sold repeatedly.

NOTE: The dark web is a real and dangerous place. I do NOT recommend you go looking for it or many of the things I discuss here. Not only can this make you a specific target to this close-knit group, but just taking part in a conversation on a web form may be considered illegal.

How Are Your Credentials Exposed?

So, how do your credentials and personal information end up on the dark web? Through data breaches, phishing scams, and ransomware, of course.

One example of a data breach is the 2017 Equifax one which exposed the personal information of over 143 million Americans. This data included names, addresses, email addresses, driver's licenses, and other sensitive financial information.

Another great example is the Yahoo data breach which occurred back in 2014. Cybercriminals obtained millions of pieces of information, including Yahoo email accounts which could be used to send phishing emails on your behalf or even compromised and used to perpetrate other fraud and scams.

In the case of both of those breaches, it took time before the breaches were discovered and reported. The Yahoo data breach was not made known publicly for two years! The data had already been shared on the dark web during that time.

You might wonder what the value of your credentials has. Data auctioned on the dark web can go for $1-$8 per record. Considering that data breaches can contain millions of records, the amount to be earned by repeatedly selling this data is staggering.

Here are the most common ways your credentials are exposed.

Phishing, that is, emails disguised as legitimate communications and designed to trick users into disclosing credentials or delivering malware that captures those credentials, is still at the top of the list.

Malvertising is a technique where malware is installed on legitimate websites through advertising networks. As a result, visitors can have credentials captured before the website owners, or advertising network realizes the code has been installed.

Another tactic, known as watering holes, targets social media and corporate sites to deliver malware in the same way as above. Social medial sites such as Facebook are also used to collect data through software, games, and false friend requests. All of these use social engineering to trick users into divulging sensitive data. Games on Facebook may seem innocent enough, asking you to name a favorite band from the '80s or your high school nickname or first car. However, when you stop and consider this, you answer common security questions that might expose your bank accounts.

Since criminals use automated software to scan the Internet for vulnerabilities on websites, servers, small business networks, and any other device or computer with an Internet connection, unpatched software or computers are a common entry point to further access our credentials and data.

Recently a vulnerability in Microsoft's email product (Exchange) exposed servers to criminals, giving them access to a company's entire email history, including emails, contacts, calendar items, and tasks. Left unpatched, this vulnerability poses a serious security threat to companies of all sizes still using that software.

In short, cybercriminals are talented at tricking us into divulging credentials and sensitive data. As a result, the risk of your exposed credentials being bought, sold, and traded on the dark web is tremendous. Once exposed, those credentials can be used to create and deliver ransomware, expand the phishing scam to those in your address book, or gain access to your other accounts and services, including financial accounts.

What are Stolen Credentials Used For?

The most common question regarding cybersecurity is, "Are the bad guys *really* after *me*?" That's usually followed up by a statement such as "I'm so small" or "I don't have anything anyone would want to steal," and "I'm not a doctor or lawyer or attorney" or any other industry that they feel is more prone to these types of data breaches.

First, yes, we are all at risk regardless of the size of our businesses, even yours. It doesn't matter if you're one person or 100 people company. Your personal information and the data you store are valuable to the bad guys for many reasons.

First, data is traded and sold on the dark web in auction and shopping sites all day long. Advertisements such as "10,000 verified email addresses and passwords" and "USA Business and Investor Database 8 Million Records" or even "300 x Business owners" are the headlines used to advertise the database of information they have collected.

Since we are talking about very tech-savvy individuals, this exchange of information can easily be combined with other data from other data breaches and other sources to build a complete profile about you, your company, or your customers.

The apparent initial use of your credentials is to sell them to others. Depending on the amount of data collected, credentials can sell for a few cents to several dollars each and repeatedly resold. For example, suppose you consider a database of usernames and passwords with email addresses might sell for $8.00 per record. In that case, anyone able to collect a few thousand records now has an impressive product to sell. Enough to make a great living.

Your credentials are also used for other nefarious means as well.

Identity theft. The more data collected about you, the easier it is to begin using that data to commit identity theft. This is advertised on the dark web by using the term "FULLZ," signifying that there is enough data to do so.

Email spoofing. Spammers can send emails on your behalf with your email address and name alone. Combine that with any of the contacts in your email account, and they now can better trick people you know into providing sensitive information since the emails appear to be from you.

Suppose the criminals can gain credentials for your email account, which frequently happens with Yahoo! and other free accounts. In that case, they can now actually log into your account and communicate directly with your friends and colleagues! And, they are clever enough to clean up after themselves, deleting traces of those email conversations and their activity. Further, since they can access your email, they can mimic your voice and writing style. I've seen this scam go on for days or weeks without the victims being any wiser for it, leading to someone sending additional credentials or even wiring money to someone they believe is their friend.

Consider, if nothing else, that a threat actor can target you for additional phishing attacks with your email address. You now become a known potential victim. The thing to consider with ransomware is what would be the effect to you and your business if you lost access to all your information? What if the proposals, writings, presentations, and all the documents you owned were suddenly inaccessible? This is the ransomware threat. For most people, their data, at the very least, is important to them. Ransomware plays on that importance.

Your credentials can also be used to access other accounts. One example was the launch of the Disney+ streaming service. Upon launch, Disney reported attacks on the service. Original news reports implied that the hackers attempted to access the service backend. However, it turns out that the hackers were merely trying the millions of email addresses and passwords that they had collected from other sources and previous data breaches in hopes that you had reused a password to sign up for this new service as well. Once an account was verified as active, it was sold on the dark web for as little as $3.00 each. (NY POST)

The size of your company does not matter as it's your credentials and information that are of real value. Of course, your personal information, email, and passwords are the bare minimum that threat actors are hoping to get from you. But, armed with even these few pieces of information, they can hold you for further ransom or as the beginning of a more extensive profile for sale to others or perpetrate other crimes.

Your data is important to you. Your credentials are keys to unlocking so many things in today's Internet world. And, it's valuable to the bad guys as well.

Humans: The Targets and the Defense

When you picked up this book, you may have thought that all I would talk about was the technical stuff. You probably expected this thing to be full of jargon and a slew of things that you may even be afraid would be over your head.

But listen, here's the deal: This book is about you, a human being, a business owner, and someone who's worried about cybersecurity and protecting their data.

I mean, if you're watching the news at all, it's full of reports of the bad guys getting access to our personal information through our computer systems, systems we've come to rely upon to run our businesses.

I don't know about you, but as a small business owner myself, this kind of stuff scares the crap out of me.

You may even wonder if all the stuff on the news could happen to you. After all, why would those bad guys want anything you have? Of course, you're small potatoes compared to a government, city, or police department, aren't you?

I think ransomware today is, on a scale of 1-10, now at an 11. Why do I say that? Because we rely on business networks. I'm frightened by the range and breadth of capabilities available and the huge financial rewards available to bad actors.

And, these attacks are coming directly at you, but they're coming from a variety of other vectors as well.

All of your vendors, for example, have the potential to be hacked, exposing some of your data. We call these supply-chain attacks.

It's economics. It's easier to extort money from small businesses when compared to larger companies.

Ransomware is prevalent. It's sophisticated. And the bad guys are constantly developing more sophisticated business models for attacking small businesses. It's real.

Hundreds, if not thousands, of small businesses are ransomware victims. Now, if you go searching for statistics on just how many businesses fall victim to ransomware and other cyberattacks, you'll see numbers all over the place. Sixty percent. Ninety percent. Fifty percent. But you know what? It's always some big number of companies going under after a ransomware attack.

Why don't you see the newspaper full of reports about little guys like you?

When something happens every day, all day long, it's not newsworthy, right?

For example, as autopilot vehicles are developed and become available, an accident in one of those vehicles becomes headline news! But it may be one of 20 thousand other accidents in other vehicles. These just aren't newsworthy.

The second reason is that ransomware and data breaches can damage small businesses. So, of course, the CPA firm down the street that suffers an attack will do everything possible to hide that and not make it public.

You may think that because I'm an IT guy, I will focus only on the technical aspects of dealing with ransomware. However, we will talk a lot in this short book about the human element of protecting your data and network from bad guys.

But you know, all this technology we are using is built by humans. We aren't perfect. Therefore, the software and systems we use aren't perfect either.

One of my pet peeves is when something goes wrong, and someone says it was a "computer glitch." Bull$h!+! It started with humans, we built it, and the mistakes always come back to humans.

The other thing is that technology can only go so far and solve so many problems. We're the ones that make mistakes and click the wrong links.

Do bad actors find a way to get in through a bug or infiltrate a security system? Of course, they do. But the number one way they get into your systems is phishing.

Some cons start with an email, and they follow up with a phone call. Even professionals can fall for these scams.

Ultimately, training and processes are the keys.

Section II: Protecting Your Small Business

Rating Your Company's Technological Maturity

Ok, so what the heck does "Technological Maturity" mean? And what does it have to do with cybersecurity?

Your company's technological maturity level tells me how you view technology and its role in your company. It is a simple breakdown of the three most common attitudes I find small business owners have about technology.

These attitudes tell me a lot about how seriously you may treat security issues and how you budget your company's human and financial resources when it comes to that technology.

I look at your company's Technological Maturity as a pyramid. At the base of that pyramid are most companies I run into.

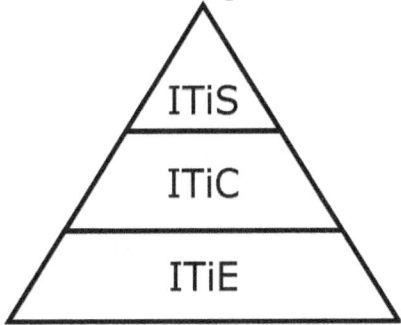

ITIE: IT is Evil. I hate technology. I'm going to do everything as cheaply as I can. I'm not concerned about getting infected or ransomware. Companies at this level are not strategic. They probably aren't growing.

The owner is frazzled, or maybe a startup, and he's doing things himself. Maybe he's got some 'guy' helping him with things. This is the business that sees IT as Evil. And that's the foundation.

You know, it amazes me when I talk to small businesses that most owners will tell me that they couldn't run their business without their computer systems. Even owners at this level get angry when technology fails or doesn't work as they hoped. And yet, companies at this level treat it like something to be shunned or avoided. They treat it like a commodity or an expense instead of an investment.

I find that these companies will not apply anything I've talked about here today. Yeah, they might go ahead and install some antivirus applications on their computers. Sure, they may outsource a task or two, but there's nothing proactive here. There's nothing strategic about how they view their IT, and thinking strategically about your IT can not only help streamline and protect your business, but it can help it grow and flourish and help make your company into the best version of itself that you can make it.

Businesses at this level have the "we're too small to be hacked" attitude towards cybersecurity. They are more than willing to use a HOPE strategy for their security; they ignore it and "hope we don't have an issue." As you know, hope is not a strategy. Especially when it comes to security, this type of business focuses on putting out fires instead of preventing them.

The next level is ITiC. The second level is a little smaller, and it's the next level that companies reach in their business's overall growth. ITiC stands for IT is a Cost. They never want to invest in what they're doing. They realize technology's importance, but it's costly and treated like the same type of commodity as the phone or chair or desk in the office. If we don't have to replace it, let's not, even if it costs us productivity or opens us up to cyber threats because we're not taking proactive steps to prevent it.

This group is starting to grow and mature in their business but is still convinced that they are the experts and can do it themselves. ITiC companies are beginning to learn the value and long-term savings of proactive maintenance and strategic planning but still aren't quite there yet. They aren't strategic yet. They likely have an IT company they work with when something breaks but do little to prevent issues from happening in the first place.

The final tier on the pyramid, and the smallest too, is the top. That's the ITiS level. IT Is Strategic. These types of companies are profitable and growing like gangbusters. They are proactive people who update their business plans quarterly!

You focus on what you do well and outsource everything else at this level. When I run across these companies, they are ready to create well-thought-out plans about how technology will help them grow their businesses.

These organizations are also ready to invest in their cybersecurity because they realize that working proactively to prevent a business-crippling disaster makes a whole darn lot of sense!

The ITiS level, and I believe since you're reading this book it includes you, are people that see IT as an investment, not a cost center. Not something evil. These people have a strong partnership with IT experts and may even outsource it to an IT partner like Cyberstreams.

Defense in Depth

When it comes to protecting your small business, I often talk about Napoleon. Back in his day, you would line up two rows of soldiers, and someone would yell, "Ready. Aim. Fire!" and they would let a volley of bullets fly at each other.

Later, they realized that if you broke your army up into groups, hid behind a hill, and fought on multiple fronts, you could frustrate your enemy—this approach to war allowed even smaller armies to defeat larger troops.

Defense in Depth (DiD) applies this concept to technology. First, we ask, "how many different things can we do to protect your data?" Then, we build layers of security into the solution so that if the bad guys get through the first line of defense, there are six more they have to go through.

Another way to envision DiD is as if you were a king or queen trying to protect your treasure. In this case, though, the treasure is all your data. You would build a great big castle with soldiers stationed on the walls. You'd add a moat and a drawbridge to cut off any attackers. Each layer is independent of the other and yet needs to be overcome before an army can reach the treasure room.

Below is an example of a DiD defense plan we might design for your business. You'll notice that each consecutive ring protects a different part of your network, covering you from multiple angles.

I know that this is a technical illustration, and that's what an IT company can help you understand and develop a plan to protect your data. See how each part of the chart, the plan, encompasses the next and covers multiple sides?

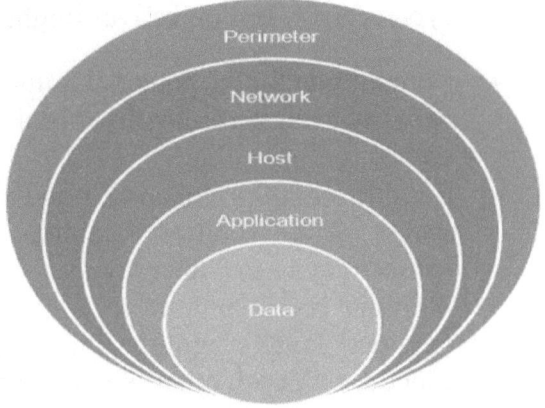

We'll look at some tools you can include in your arsenal against the bad guys in an upcoming chapter.

One of the most critical components of any security solution you want to use in your business is the human layer.

We can talk all day long about the technology, tools, and barriers that an IT company can install in your business. Still, unless you have someone, a human set of eyes, watching these, systems are eventually defeated, and you won't even know about it until it's too late.

Unlike focusing on just a purely technical solution, DiD considers humans. The defence in depth principle is traditionally interpreted as meaning that there are multiple physical layers surrounding the hazard source. However, security specialists have begun to adopt a more conceptual interpretation of the principle, which includes non-physical layers of defence such as emergency response and human and organizational factors. This broader interpretation is more effective in ensuring security. (Marsden, 2018)

DiD's objectives are:

- Make compensation for the potential failure of the systems' components or any mistake made by human errors.
- Keep the effectiveness of defense layers by averting damage to the plant and the layers themselves.
- Guard the public domains and environment against being harmed if the layers are ineffective.

Applying these principles instead to the virtual world, and your data, applying DiD to cybersecurity our objectives might look like this:

- Compensate for the potential failure of the hardware, or software systems, or any mistake made by human errors.
- Build layers of protection around your data to block access from multiple points, and to provide redundancy to the other layers.
- Multiple layers protect the data in the case of a previous layer's failure. Layers should work in concert with each other whenever possible

When it comes to your business' cybersecurity, don't rely on just one layer of protection. Implementing defense in depth (DiD) principles will help ensure that your data is safe from multiple attack points. Using various techniques, including human oversight, you can create a layered security system that is much more difficult to penetrate.

In the next couple of chapters, we'll discuss more ways you can strengthen your human security layer.

Awareness: YOUR Small Business Defense

Guess what? As hard as we're working on adding new layers of security and creating additional ways to frustrate the bad guys, they're working just as hard to figure out how to thwart us.

In my heart of hearts, I know that of all the layers we are working with today, two are the most effective. We'll discuss Multi-Factor authentication (MFA) in an upcoming chapter. That's the second most effective defense that you can put in place right now.

The first is awareness! I can't overstate enough how important awareness is in your fight against cybercriminals. No matter how many layers of technology we put in your network, the bad guys are working just as hard no matter what we do. So, things get through any solution. I wish I could tell you that we could implement something that was one-hundred percent effective all the time.

But, it's a constant back-and-forth between security and hackers, so we have to teach your staff how to be aware. Be skeptical and be afraid. Be paranoid about everything.

We're finding now that the threat actors, the bad guys, are working diligently to circumvent every technological barrier and layer of security we put in place.

They are targeting your people. Your staff. Us. The hackers cast a wide net and try to trap your people into making a mistake.

You must build your team's awareness of all the ways that your data can be released or exposed.

The other thing is that without proper training on how to use the technology, your chances of a data breach increase, just from someone making a mistake—for example, clicking on "Send" without encrypting a sensitive email—entering credentials into a phishing website. These behaviors threaten your business just as much, if not more, than a failure in the technology itself.

Creating a Cybersecurity Culture

I've discussed the human aspect of cybersecurity a lot. As an organization, though, you continuously want to improve your cybersecurity safety culture.

Building a culture takes buy-in from all levels of your company, not just the IT Department.

Your staff needs to know that you take your cybersecurity seriously and that their behaviors affect security as much as the technology in place does.

Phishing and social engineering are increasing in frequency and aggressiveness because they work, and they work by taking advantage of us as human beings.

Security is complicated and inconvenient. People don't like passwords and multi-factor authentication because they are time-consuming, adding extra steps to the work they need to complete.

But you must reinforce the message that these are essential things that all employees at all levels need to be aware of.

It helps if you implement regular training courses and discuss your security regularly.

Here are some tips for creating a cybersecurity culture in your company.

- Use a password manager and only allow password sharing when needed. Passwords should never be shared in texts or emails. Instead, use the password manager's sharing feature to do this. Also, as we discuss in the zero trust model, you need to make sure that people only have access to the passwords they need. Passwords are the first line of defense in so many ways. Remembering is hard. Even with a good password manager, people are tempted to take shortcuts. Sticky notes, the paper under the keyboard, and reusing passwords are probably the most common security violations we see.

- Frequent reminders and discussions are necessary to keep your culture of security top of mind. Security is an evolving topic, and this type of discussion should not be a one-and-done event. To truly build your culture, have regular conversations and reminders about this.

- Engage your team in regular training. This can be done via a paid service, such as the one you might get from an IT company like Cyberstream. Services such as this may even include sample phishing tests.

Here is a three-step plan you and your IT team can implement:

1. Enable Single Sign-On for any important applications that accept it. Single sign-on is when you can use one ID and password to log in to many different online systems. This way, you do not need to remember every system's information, eliminating the need for users to remember different passwords and ensuring that access (or removal) is managed in M365 (or Google or whatever) alongside user accounts and company regulations.
2. Enable MFA everywhere it's available. This makes the risk of a breach so low it's nearly zero. So require this on every website, software program, mobile device, and computer system that you possibly can.
3. Enforce the importance of passwords and password hygiene. After enabling MFA and Single Sign-On, users won't need to remember and change passwords as frequently. However, teaching staff that they still need to avoid their old, insecure habits like writing passwords on sticky notes or in spreadsheets and creating passwords out of the old password reduces the effectiveness of the password and makes security more frustrating for everyone.

Cybersecurity is not a topic anyone usually associates with company culture. But, it has to be treated with the same respect as being a team player and living up to other company values.

Begin by adding items from the list and discussing them frequently. Whenever possible, try to make your discussions on cybersecurity short, specific, and fun.

We've talked about how much the bad guys love to use our emails for scams and phishing schemes. I got tired of repeating the same things about checking attachments and not clicking on links.

That's where "**S.L.A.M.**" came in. SLAM was my way of making this teaching moment more memorable. I recently had the opportunity to have this chat with a neighbor

My neighbor looked distraught and asked my advice because her dad had just fallen for a phishing scam. She was nearly about to cry. She had spent all day closing accounts and locking his credit ratings.

I gave her my SLAM Talk.

"Let's SLAM that email!"

"S: Does the sender's email address look strange, not who you expect? Don't open that email!

"L: Are there links? Hover over them. Do they have some strange address? Wells Fargo isn't going to send an email from welllsflargo.com. Don't click!"

"A: Are there attachments? Hackers love to embed dangerous stuff in attachments. Unless you know good and well that Bob is sending you an attachment, then trash it!

"M: Read the message. Is the English just a little bit off? Is there a space before a period? Then just slam that email! Hit delete!"

My neighbor walked away, repeating my mantra, "Slam that Email!"

Cybersecurity doesn't have to be boring, and folding it into your culture is critical in today's environment. Look for creative and fun ways to train your team, such as explainer videos, infographics, or short tutorials. Many companies also provide regular testing and training. If something like this interests you, Cyberstreams has a service that does just that.

Multi-Factor Authentication: Your New Best Friend

I mentioned earlier that, apart from awareness and training, I believe that Multi-Factor Authentication (MFA) is the second most crucial layer of protection you can have in your defense arsenal right now.

You've probably used MFA before. Right now, most banks and online shopping platforms have some sort of extra authentication in place to prove you are who you say you are when you log into their sites. When you log into your account, you're asked for a username and password, but then a second form of proof (authentication) that you are authorized to access the account.

Multi-Factor Authentication includes two things:

First is something you know, such as your username and password.

The second is something you have. This can be a code that gets texted to your cell phone or an app. It can even be something like a fingerprint or biometric data.

We are now encouraging our clients to move away from text messages for the second form of authentication because it is possible to spoof your cell phone. It's not a secure means of communicating. Also, while rare, if a hacker can gain access to other parts of your identity, they can contact the cell company and get them to change your account or even get a sim card, allowing them to take over your cell phone and intercept your phone messages.

We recommend, instead, the use of an authenticator app on your cell phone. There are several of them out there. They are easy to download and install. This layer of security is so important and easy to do that there's no excuse for not doing it. Microsoft and Google both have authenticator apps that work with nearly any website that uses MFA.

Requiring an employee to use their cell phone for MFA does have challenges. For example, many manufacturers don't allow phones on the production floor, or employees who aren't given a company-owned phone are resistant to letting us install an app. So, what do you do in cases like this?

Well, we've been using more hardware-based devices just for these reasons. These have been around for quite a while now, but with the need for MFA nearly everywhere, they are becoming more popular again.

These items are usually called a Key or FOB. These hardware identification devices with a rotating number on them, changing every 30 seconds, just like the phone apps do. The difference is you just carry the device around with you. They can also take the form of a USB stick that you plug into your computer to allow you access the device, network, or online resource you need. Without the device, you cannot get in. One company that makes a device like this is YubiKey.

These devices store an encrypted password and require that you enter a PIN on the computer when you insert them and then touch the device. This makes them virtually un-hackable.

Cyber Resilience

There are a couple of new approaches and ways of thinking about cybersecurity and how we defend ourselves against the bad guys. It's tough out there right now. But, as I've mentioned, a lot of your cybersecurity approach, especially if you're a manufacturer or small business, is with the human component.

I've said it before, and I'll repeat it, that awareness and education are at the top of my list for keeping your company safe.

There's also this realization in the industry that we continue fighting this back-and-forth war between our two sides.

The first step in becoming cyber resilient is to assume you will be hacked. The change is from thinking about whether you'll get hacked to contemplating when you will experience a breach. This method helps you create a strategy for your small business's recovery following a breach (resilience) of all its defenses. What then?

That's where cyber resilience steps in. It's a strategy for the worst-case scenario. This method does not imply that you have established all of your defensive lines. Of course, you're giving yourself up to an assault without them. Cyber resilience theory is there to guide you through what you'll do when you are attacked, rather than how to prevent it.

I recently bought this little sailboat. Mine has a sealed compartment in the front and the back, and these are filled with Styrofoam. The Coast Guard requires that you have positive flotation on a boat like that. Positive flotation is when the manufacturer puts enough material in the boat so that, even with a hull breach, the boat will float.

Now, you hope you're never going to need that, right? I mean, you aren't hoping for a hull breach. But, when it happens, you sure want to know that you have enough positive flotation to keep you above water until you can get back to shore and patch your hull.

This is what cyber resilience is. It's planning for the worst so that if it happens, you know how to bounce back and get your business up and running as quickly as possible.

When working on a resiliency plan, you may include things like your backups.

Prevention AND cure have to be part of your cybersecurity plan.

Six Cybersecurity Tips Any Small Business Can Implement

When a business owner comes to me and says, "We're tiny, just a few people, and I can't afford to hire IT right away," then these are the first things I tell them. Anyone can establish simple precautions like these by either learning to do it themselves or working with an external IT company for a one-time cost with regular quarterly check-ins to ensure things are still going well. If you focus on only a few key security elements, to begin with, you'll improve your overall security in no time.

For example, I can't tell you how many times I've spoken to solo or small businesses who haven't even changed the default password on the router. So when you grab something like a router off the shelf at the store, bring it home or into your office, and plug it in without even changing the default password, you're just inviting the bad guys in because you haven't done anything to keep them out.

Here are the six cybersecurity steps you can implement right now:

1. Be mindful. Be aware. This is really what creating a cybersecurity culture is all about. We need people to pause in our hectic, fast-paced work environment. Stop and think about the email you are replying to. Think before you click on that link. Think before you open an attachment. Awareness is what it's all about. The bad guys figure out ways to get around our technology and security.

2. At a minimum, use antivirus software. It's only about 30% effective, but it's better than nothing. But you have to realize that you are exposed.

3. Make a backup of your data. I always tell people to back up their data, but it's more than that. It's all about having a plan in place to protect your data. For example, I had a hospital client who had backup tapes. They were religious about swapping out these backup tapes and putting them in the vault. But, one day, their system went down. So they pulled out the tapes hoping to restore their data, and the tapes were empty! They had never tested them.

4. Passwords: I highly recommend using a password manager. LastPass is a popular choice. I can have one really strong password for LastPass, and LastPass will ensure I have unique, complex passwords for everything else. Use complex passwords and never

reuse the same passwords for anything. Don't ever, ever leave the default password for anything. Change the password for every device. Default passwords are well documented and easy to hack.

5. MFA. Apart from education and training, multi-factor authentication is probably the easiest, least expensive, and quickest security strategy you can implement right now. So turn MFA on everywhere, and I mean everywhere, you and your team can.

6. Device Security: Keeping every device up to date and patched. Configuring your firewalls correctly. Limiting rights and putting in controls to stop users from installing malicious software. Ensuring that every computer and device that connects to your software uses the latest software and security updates. If you're small, usually under ten computers, this can be done with a weekly check by someone on your staff. However, it can almost become a full-time position once you get to about ten computers. At that point, I recommend that you talk with an IT company about managing patches and updates for you.

So these are just six things that you can go and do right now. Next, let's look at some slightly more advanced steps I recommend.

7 Cost-Effective Advanced Security Steps

As your company grows and matures, you will need to add additional layers of security. The seven I list below are slightly more advanced than those in the previous chapter but are well worth it to protect you and your customers' data.

For these seven items, you will likely need to reach out to an IT company such as Cyberstreams to help you implement these. However, once implemented, they become maintenance items.

1. Network threat detection: I mentioned a few times that we are constantly working to protect your data as IT professionals. Unfortunately, at the same time, but bad guys are working to circumvent everything we do to get at your data. For example, to hack your network and hold you for ransom. That's why I recommend you work with an IT professional to set up some sort of network threat detection. This is software that sits on your network and monitors for suspicious activity. Since the threat actors are busy trying to quietly get through your systems, you need some sort of guardian watching what's going on in your network and looking for things out of the ordinary. This allows you to react quickly instead of being surprised by ransomware after it's too late.
2. Cloud protection and monitoring: I've mentioned that, overall, when you work with a reputable cloud company, such as Microsoft or Amazon Web Services, to host your data, you are partnering with someone who has infinitely more security resources than you do. But, that doesn't mean that you should be complacent. Microsoft 365 accounts, for example, are constantly being targeted. So, having someone set up monitoring these accounts for you, looking for suspicious activities, is another layer of security I heavily recommend. Usually provided by an IT company, these services watch for unusual access to your accounts and quickly alert you to a potential issue.
3. Email message security: Some statistics state that as much as 90% of the malware and ransomware that infects small

businesses still comes from email, and I believe it. This is the easiest way for the bad guys to target you. You can build a culture of "trust but verify" when it comes to email, but ultimately you want a software filtering program to have your back. Software filtering does more than fight the spammers. It also can help with phishing schemes and links to malicious websites. Plus, depending on what you use, email security can encrypt communications between you and your clients and even automatically encrypt data that may accidentally be exposed. For example, suppose someone includes a password or social security number in an email but forgets to click the "encrypt" button. In that case, the software can do it automatically.

4. Business continuity: Business continuity is more than having a good backup. It's about how quickly you can have your business back up and running when something does happen. It's about keeping your business running in the face of a disaster, whether that's a natural disaster like a fire or flood or a network disaster such as a ransomware attack or hardware or software failure. Today it even includes thinking about keeping your business running if the Internet goes out. Sit down with your IT professional and review your current setup. They can recommend adding simple redundancies and point out potential continuity pitfalls.

5. Encryption: There are a few things that must be encrypted. First, any secure communications that might include Personally Identifiable Information (PII). See my email encryption step above. But you also need to encrypt your backups and devices, especially mobile devices such as laptops, tablets, and phones. For example, suppose a laptop containing sensitive information is lost. In that case, its data can easily be accessed by a professional unless the hard drive has been encrypted. This can usually be turned on in the Operating System, so it's not difficult to implement. The benefit here is that it's not a data breach if the device is stolen but encrypted since it cannot be accessed.

6. Data destruction: This gets overlooked a lot. You need to think about what you do with your equipment when you retire it. This goes for hard drives, computes, USB drives, or anything that may have data on it. Even copiers and scanners store data and should be wiped by a professional before they are donated, disposed of, or passed along.
7. Training: Although last in this list, it's undoubtedly one of the most important facets of security for you to implement. When your company reaches ten employees or more, you should step up your education and awareness efforts by partnering with a third party to provide this service. You want to ensure that; a) you aren't the one managing it, b) that the service includes some reporting, and c) it is occurring at least monthly.

So these are the seven additional advanced tips that I want you to implement as your company grows. Layering these components on top of whatever you have in place now, and working with a quality IT Partner, will go a long way towards protecting you and your customers' data.

Zero Trust

Zero trust is a pretty darn simple concept, and the name almost gives it away. But it's not "zero" trust. Instead, it's a cybersecurity methodology that has this pretense:

"Trust nothing without verification and approval."

You start with not trusting anything or anybody and then approving what they can do and what they can access when they need it and request it.

For example, twenty years ago, when a new employee started, we would have given them full access to everything in our systems. Now we start with only the bare necessities to get them up and running. They lack access to specific tools, financial reports, and even software.

And then, when down the road, they come back and say, "I can't do this thing." There's an evaluation. Does that employee truly need access to that thing? Or do they need to request that thing be done by somebody else so that we limit the number of people who can do the thing?

It's not zero trust. It's metered or measured trust. Zero trust is just a convenient way to say, "this is the starting point." Trust nothing until we know we should trust a little. And then we slowly trust a little more and then a little more after that.

This is something that even a small business of just a couple of employees can implement because it's a way of thinking about security and doesn't always require a lot of fancy IT work. A lot of this comes down to business processes.

Let's take an example of a small CPA firm just starting. Let's say it's just you and your spouse at first. Maybe you have access to everything: bank accounts, client accounts, etc.

But then, you add your third employee, someone from outside. Are you going to immediately give this brand-new person access to your checkbook if his job has nothing to do with banking? What about all your accounts and financial information? If his job has nothing to do with banking, why would you give him a username and password to your banking site? If he's not going to write checks, why would you unlock your cabinet and hand him 100 checks?

You wouldn't do that. I hope you wouldn't do that!

So, why can't we apply this same logic to everything, even our computer systems? The answer is we can, and that's what zero trust is all about.

Now, at some point, I'm still going to recommend that you discuss some of the more technical decisions with an IT company like Cyberstream. It's not always cut-and-dried on how to apply these types of permissions. For example, sometimes, we run into a piece of software that everyone in the company may need to use that won't run without giving someone more permissions than you'd initially want to.

But these are the types of things that we regularly review with our clients and discuss during our IT Planning Meetings. These are strategic conversations about how your business runs and how to mitigate your risk. Often it's simply a matter of not giving people access to a piece of software at all.

It's about being aware.

I'll give you an example of something we do in our business. We have an office manager who can pay vendors and write checks. But we have a process for this. We don't write paper checks. We do it through our online bank. So, he can go online and issue payments. But his permissions won't allow him to create additional users.

But, before he can issue a payment, we review this during our weekly meeting. First, submit which payments they want to make. Then we have a real conversation, not a text or email, to review the payments. I then approve the appropriate ones. Only then does he process those payments. Once done, I get an alert from my bank that they are scheduled.

This is an example of the checks and balances built into this process. They prevent my office manager from moving my funds around without my specific approval.

I tell many people that the first place to start is to guard your money. Make a precise and detailed process and ensure your employees follow it.

When we talk about a threat like phishing, we describe a specific set of procedures that bad people use to try and con you. Many phishing exercises try and fool you into getting access to your money.

Imagine a pretty, young woman walks into a gas station, distraught at losing her wedding ring. In the end, she gains the trust of the gas station attended and scams him out of a bunch of money.

Tricking humans has been around for millennia. It's the con! It's about Social Engineering.

Social Engineering is what con artists and bad guys do. They use psychological manipulation to get their victim to take the desired action. Social engineering, however, no longer needs to be in person like our story above. Instead, it happens all the time to people over the Internet. It happens through emails and phone calls, and now even text messages.

Let me ask, "If you were walking down the street and spotted a quarter, would you bend over and pick it up? I would.

If you look across the traffic and see a twenty-dollar bill, would you dart through traffic and go after those twenty dollars? I would."

At what point do you stop taking a risk? How much are you willing to risk? How much money is that you'd want to lose? What is that number? And only you can answer that. So, the human checks and balances and the zero trust are how we avoid this.

When this comes to ransomware, it's usually delivered via email and tricking someone into clicking a link that takes them somewhere and convincingly fools your staff into revealing private information such as accounts and credentials

Constantly and persistently talking to your staff about security. You have to treat each email as an attack. This is how we use zero trust to fight against ransomware.

The challenge with ransomware is that it attacks your organization from all sides. It attacks your people directly and attacks the technological barriers and security you put into place.

This is why the zero trust security model is becoming a powerful tool against these attacks.

Here are some examples of things you might put into place as part of a zero trust security plan. Note that none of these alone is enough.

- Protect emails by filtering them before they hit your inbox.
- Use URL filtering and protection to review websites and only allow those that have passed your filtering rules.
- Use the most restrictive account settings on your computers for your users. For example, only those with administrative rights should install and change the software. This helps prevent malware

from getting installed accidentally and requires someone to approve it, not allowing it to get silently installed in the background.
- Implement checks and balances for everything, including accessing your funds, accounts, and network resources. Only approve access when it's requested, and then review it. You might ask:
  - Does the person need access to this resource?
  - Is this the right person to give access to, or should you assign the task to someone else?
  - Should access to the resource be temporary?

You might be thinking that zero trust might not be a good fit for your small business. Still, you can implement this in your organization, regardless of its size.

How Many Berries Do You Have Stored Up?

There's a lot in this book that's scary, right? I mean, we're talking about outside forces, which you probably don't get, attacking your business and stealing from you.

It's most likely why you picked up this book. You're worried about your business. The current state of ransomware and cyber threats certainly don't help. But, I'm here to tell you something.

Worry and fear are tools.

These are part of our human nature. We can completely ignore those warning signs or pay attention to them strategically and constructively.

Worry is the part of us that used to help us gather and store enough berries to make it through the winter. Fear ensures you don't get eaten by a bear while doing it.

This is where we've been for millennium. It's healthy to have some fear and worry. It's healthy to seek security. It's healthy to implement some security guards.

We have car insurance because we worry about what might happen if we get into an accident. You make sure that your vehicle is in good shape and that it has airbags, seatbelts, and properly inflated tires because all those things, those layers of security, protect you when you're driving. They help you if something does happen by potentially reducing the damage or injury from an accident. We all know that these things are intelligent things to do and, if we do them, it helps us sleep just a little bit easier.

Well, there are all kinds of bad guys out there trying to steal your money and trick your employees. They want your berries and will eat you to get them!

So, when we bring this back to cybersecurity, and the ITiS people, then having a bit of fear and worry about the state of your cybersecurity is a natural and healthy reaction to protecting your valuable business assets.

So, leverage this fear and worry to create a plan and implement a cybersecurity culture in your company.

Doing business with the DOD

The Department of Defense is making it more difficult for potential attackers to access sensitive data or systems by requiring contractors to meet rigorous cybersecurity requirements. The Cybersecurity Maturity Model Certification (CMMC) will also help ensure that defense contractors protect their data.

The Department of Defense has long required that its contractors have robust cybersecurity protections. This requirement, known as CMMC, is new, but it builds on an existing regulation (DFARS) that has been in place for several years.

Previously, contractors could self-certify their compliance with NIST cybersecurity standards. However, CMMC will now require third-party validation to prove compliance.

The goal of CMMC is to improve the cybersecurity posture of defense contractors and reduce the risk of cyberattacks. By requiring contractors to meet rigorous cybersecurity requirements, the DoD makes it more difficult for potential attackers to access sensitive data or systems.

Cyberstreams is a Seattle-based IT company that has helped many of our clients to meet the cybersecurity requirements needed to take on work for the Department of Defense. For example, suppose you are a current or future Defense Industrial Base (DIB) contractor, a subcontractor, or any business in the supply chain that might touch the DoD's sensitive data. In that case, you have a dizzying array of rules and regulations to manage. I've included just a few highlights on what you need to consider in the following pages.

Who Cares About the DoD DFARS/CMMC/NIST 800-171?

As you probably know, anyone doing business or working on a subcontractor basis with another company that holds a federal government contract needs to meet all cybersecurity requirements.

The problem is that the Department of Defense (DoD) has been changing the rules around cybersecurity constantly, so it's hard to keep up.

Working with an IT company specializing in helping their clients meet stringent cybersecurity requirements needed to do business with the DoD can benefit your business in quickly achieving these requirements.

It can be hard to understand which ones apply to you and your business with so many certifications and requirements. Be sure you are working with a trusted partner who knows these cybersecurity standards and applies them to a company like yours.

Why CMMC, DFARS, and NIST 800-171?

The media and the general public are becoming more aware of cyber espionage. Hackers and foreign governments on the Internet steal government and commercial secrets. They're also aggressively attacking businesses and outsourced contractors to access government data.

The Peoples' Republic of China aims to become the ONLY superpower. Let that sink in! Other nations consider us their enemy as well. The Chinese air force flies jets and operates factories that are nearly exact replicas of US designs. These nations have and continue to steal our national secrets.

With the new push for better security, the DoD increases its cybersecurity requirements to ensure accountable contractors. Companies working with federal government contractors need to show they have met specific standards and regulations or risk losing future business opportunities with the DoD.

DRARS, NIST 800-171, and CMMC are overlapping standards and regulations designed to combat these efforts. CMMC is a more recent development that has garnered much attention in the DIB.

What is CMMC?

The Cybersecurity Maturity Model Certification (CMMC) is a unified standard for implementing cybersecurity across the Defense Industrial Base (DIB). The CMMC sets out standards that contractors must follow to secure sensitive data.

CMMC provides a training, certification, and third-party assessment framework for DIB contractors. CMMC is an evolving set of requirements that augment and overlap with The Defense Federal Acquisition Regulations Supplements (DFARS) and NIST 800-171, which dictates how defense contractors and subcontractors manage Controlled Unclassified Information (CUI).

The Department of Defense announced the first version, CMMC 1.0, in 2019. It spelled out basic cybersecurity processes and practices in a complicated model framework of 17 categories (domains) mapped across five maturity levels: basic, intermediate, good, proactive, and advanced.

Why CMMC 2.0?

CMCC 2.0 looks to reduce "red tape for small and medium-sized businesses" by cutting back the need for accreditation and reducing the number of levels to three: Foundational, Advanced, and Expert. These changes should save the average DIB contractor tens of thousands of dollars over the next several years.

What is going on with CMMC 2.0?

To achieve the Foundational level, DoD outlines 17 basic practices DIB contractors must meet and requires only self-attestation as proof of compliance. The Advanced level increases the required practices to 110, aligning with the National Institute for Standards and Technology (NIST) special publication (SP) 800-171.

CMMC 1.0 is suspended, and CMMC 2.0 is being completed and is expected within the next 24 months. Until then, it will not be a contract requirement. However, DFARS remains the law of the land, and many DIB contractors will continue to be required to adhere to NIST 800-171. The DoD is looking into ways to incentivize DIB contractors to comply with CMMC in the meantime.

So, Where Does the Rubber Meet the Road?

- CMMC is coming, and it will look a lot like DFARS 7020, but with more teeth
- DFARS 7020 is the law NOW, and breaking it could put you on the wrong side of the courtroom from a federal prosecutor
- DFARS requires a minimum of a NIST 800-171 Basic assessment and submission to SPRS; they may come back and ask for a medium or high (a much deeper look)
- DIB Contractors that are preparing now will have a competitive advantage

Section III: The Small Business Guide to Cybersecurity Implementation

Nine Minimal Steps to Better Protection

While it's impossible to plan for every potential computer problem or emergency, a little proactive monitoring and maintenance of your network will help you avoid or significantly reduce the impact of the vast majority of computer disasters you could experience.

Unfortunately, I have found that most small business owners are NOT conducting any type of proactive monitoring or maintaining their network, which leaves them utterly vulnerable to the kinds of disasters you just read about. This is primarily for three reasons:

#1. They don't understand the importance of regular maintenance.

#2. Even if they understand its significance, they simply do not know what maintenance is required or how to do it.

#3. They are already swamped with more immediate day-to-day fires demanding their attention. If their network is working fine today, it goes to the bottom of the pile of things to worry about. That means no one is watching to ensure the backups are working correctly, the virus protection is up-to-date, critical security patches are applied, or the network is "healthy" overall.

While there are hundreds of necessary daily, weekly, and monthly checks and maintenance tasks, I will share the nine most important for protecting your company.

Step #1: Make Sure You Are Backing Up Your Files

It just amazes me how many businesses never back up their computer network. Imagine this: you write the most important piece of information you could ever write on a chalkboard, and I come along and erase it. How are you going to get it back? You're not. Unless you can remember it, you can't recover the data if you made a copy of it. It's gone. That is why it is so important to back up your network. Several things could cause you to lose data files. If the information on the disk is important to you, make sure you have more than one copy of it.

Step #2: Use Only Image-Based Backups

It's no longer good enough to just backup the files that are important to you. File-only backup solutions are slow to recover because you have to reinstall and reconfigure everything from scratch before even restoring your data. Windows, software, users, mailboxes, permissions, and everything else must be set up before you are back in business again. Using an image-based solution, especially one that you can "spin up" instantly, turns this long, tedious process into one that can take as little as 20 minutes.

Step #3: Take Multiple Snapshots Throughout the Day.

The amount of data you stand to lose is directly related to the frequency of your backups. If you are only taking one backup each day, say at night, which is the most common time, then your data will only be protected at that single point in time. Disasters strike at the most inconvenient times. So, if your IT system fails at 4:30 pm, and your most recent backup is from the previous day at 11 pm, you've lost an entire day's worth of work that must be recreated! Plus, you'd better hope that you're only shot at backing up your data that night succeeded!

Step #4: Keep an Offsite Copy of Your Backups

What happens if a fire or flood destroys your server AND the backup drives? This is how hurricane Katrina devastated many businesses that have now been forced into bankruptcy. What happens if your office gets robbed and they take EVERYTHING? Having an offsite backup is simply a smart way to make sure you can get your business back up and running in a relatively short time.

Step #5: Check Your Backups Regularly To Make Sure They Are Working Properly

This is another big mistake I see. Many business owners set up some backup system but never check to ensure it's working correctly. As a result, it's not uncommon for a system to APPEAR to be backing up when it's not. There are dozens of things that can go wrong and cause your backup to become corrupt and useless. That is why it's not enough to simply back up your system. You have to check it regularly to make sure the data is recoverable in an emergency. Remember my story of the company whose data hadn't been backed up in over a month? Don't let that happen to you!

Step #6: Make Sure Your Virus Protection Is ALWAYS On AND Up-To-Date

You would have to be living under a rock to not know how devastating a virus can be to your network. With virus attacks coming from spam, downloaded data and music files, instant messages, websites, and emails from friends and clients, you cannot afford to be without up-to-date virus protection.

Not only can a virus corrupt your files and bring down your network, but it can also hurt your reputation. For example, if you or one of your employees unknowingly spreads a virus to a customer, or if the virus hijacks your email address book, you're going to make many people very angry.

Additionally, since the first thing viruses attempt to do is quietly disable your virus protection, you must constantly use monitored protection verified by a person.

Step #7: Protect Your Email from Phishing, Viruses, and Spam

Most viruses and identity theft are spread via email these days. All it takes is a single, convincing email to get a well-meaning employee to click on a link to infect your entire network.

You've seen the clever emails pretending to be someone you know and asking you to click a link or open an attachment. Once this happens, you've given these crooks "permission" to infect your network. You must have as many layers of security as possible in place. Neglecting to protect your company from the myriad of viruses spread via email is simply negligent.

Just to be clear, this filtering should not be confused with the spam filtering or junk mail folder found in your email software like Outlook. Instead, it must be a filter that checks your emails before they even arrive in your inbox.

Step #8: Set Up A Firewall

Small business owners tend to think that because they are "just a small business," no one would waste time trying to hack into their network when nothing could be further from the truth. Experiments have been conducted where a single computer is connected to the Internet with no firewall. Within hours, over 13 gigabytes of space were taken over by malicious code and files that could not be deleted. The simple fact is that there are thousands of unscrupulous individuals out there who think it's fun to disable your computer just because they can.

These individuals strike randomly by searching the Internet for open, unprotected ports. As soon as they find one, they will delete files or download huge files that cannot be deleted, shutting down your hard drive. They can also use your computer as a zombie for storing pirated software or sending spam, which will cause your ISP to shut YOU down and prevent you from accessing the Internet or sending and receiving email.

Suppose the malicious programs can't be deleted. In that case, you'll have to re-format the entire hard drive causing you to lose every piece of information you've ever owned UNLESS you were backing up your files properly (see 1 to 5 above).

Properly configured routers, access points, and software firewalls are a must. But, candidly, most that I am asked to audit are not. They haven't even had the default username and password changed! Most people working from home use inexpensive home routers let in their default settings. The bad guys can easily install spying software right on these routers. Home offices should always have a modern router that is properly configured. At a minimum, make sure the password is strong and the router is set to update its firmware automatically.

Step #9: Update Your System with Critical Security Patches as They Become Available

Suppose you do not have the most up-to-date security patches and virus definitions installed on your network. In that case, hackers can access your computer through a simple banner ad or an email attachment.

Not too long ago, Microsoft released a security bulletin about three newly discovered vulnerabilities that could allow an attacker to gain control of your computer by tricking users into downloading and opening a maliciously crafted picture. At the same time, Microsoft released a Windows update to correct the vulnerabilities. Still, if you didn't have a process to ensure you are applying critical updates as soon as they become available, you were utterly vulnerable to this attack.

Here's another compelling reason to ensure your network stays updated with the latest security patches.

Most hackers do not discover these security loopholes on their own. Instead, they learn about them when Microsoft (or any other software vendor) announces the vulnerability and issues an update. That is their cue to spring into action, and they immediately go to work analyzing the update and crafting an exploit (like a virus) that allows them access to any computer or network that has not yet installed the security patch.

Essentially, the time between the release of the update and the exploit that targets the underlying vulnerability is getting shorter every day.

When the "Nimda" worm was discovered in the fall of 2001, Microsoft had already released the patch that protected against that vulnerability almost a year before (331 days). So network administrators had plenty of time to apply the update. But, of course, many still hadn't done so, and the "Nimda" worm caused lots of damage. But in the summer of 2003, there were only 25 days between the release of the Microsoft update that would have protected against the "blaster" worm and the detection of the worm itself!

Someone needs to be paying close attention to your systems to ensure that critical updates are applied as soon as possible. That is why we highly recommend small business owners without a full-time IT staff allow their consultant to monitor and maintain their network.

The 7 Essential Layers of Security

Security is no longer an issue for large companies such as banks and financial institutions. So why are small businesses at risk now? Because they store more and more personal and confidential data, and that amount is growing day by day as we move to a paperless society.

Another reason they are at risk is that small businesses do not typically have the knowledge or the resources to dedicate to protecting their data.

I want you to think about all the sensitive data you might have and store. This doesn't necessarily have to be credit card data, social security numbers, or healthcare information. It can be Human Resources data. It can be information about your employees, client transaction data, case information, and lots of private and valuable data.

So, what's the answer to this? The solution to protecting your data as a small business is implementing layers of security. Most businesses fail in this aspect because they only have one or two layers, or they have improperly implemented the layers they have put into place, leaving their data exposed.

Each layer can be implemented cost-effectively by nearly any small business. Now, that's not to say that you shouldn't seek professional assistance to do so; I highly recommend it, but once implemented, the layers, if properly maintained, will provide a level of security that will allow you to sleep easier at night.

Let's review each of the layers.

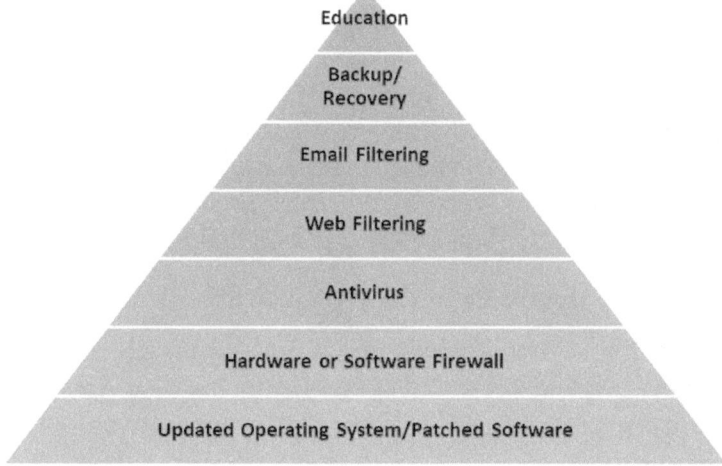

Layer # 1 – Updated and Patched Operating Systems and Software

The foundation of security is keeping your computers and software patched and updated. This includes both the operating system (like Windows) and third-party software such as your web browsers, Adobe Acrobat, and any other software running on your systems.

A properly and consistently updated system is your first line of defense.

Equifax suffered a cybersecurity breach in 2017 that exposed the personal information of 143 million Americans. The truly sad part is that the breach could have been avoided. The criminals took advantage of a known security flaw in software that Equifax was using. Even though the software manufacturer had identified and released a fix for the vulnerability three months before the breach, Equifax had failed to install the required updates.

It's estimated that unpatched vulnerabilities are the source of over 60% of data breaches (darkreading.com – 4/2018). Unpatched systems are why Windows XP is such a security risk now. Microsoft's end of support for Windows 7 and Server 2008 (both in January of 2020) is of major concern to the IT industry. Since these systems are no longer be patched, they pose a major risk to any business that still has them despite any new security issues discovered.

I'll also expose the misconception that keeping a computer with a discontinued operating system is not a risk if 'nobody uses it for surfing the Internet.' The truth of the matter is that if it's connected to your network, it poses a threat. In May of 2019, Microsoft released a security patch for Windows XP – despite XP not being supported for five years. Why? Because the vulnerability allowed hackers to access Windows 7 computers via the Windows XP machines on the network. Further, you don't have to actively be surfing the Internet on a computer for it to be discovered by cybercriminals (using automated software to scan for such computers) and attacked.

Layer #2 – Hardware or Software Firewall

Next on our list is your hardware or software firewall. This blocks holes in the network and keeps out cybercriminals. Your firewall may be handled by a router, access point, or even software on your computer.

Firewalls allow or block traffic from passing in and out of your network. For most of us, this means getting out to the Internet. For every type of traffic, we must open a port, a hole, if you will, in the firewall. Each hole then allows traffic to enter or leave the network.

The issue is that many small companies simply purchase a router from a big box store and install it with the default settings. Many don't even change the default passwords published on the Internet for anyone who wants them.

Within minutes, I can gain access to your network simply by identifying your router (easy to do with the right software) and using the default username and password.

It is best to have a properly configured router that has NOT been left with default settings.

Further, hardware devices (like routers and access points) also require software updates. We call this type of software "firmware." Why is regularly checking and updating your device's firmware important? The same reason that software patches are important.

In 2018 it was discovered that the technique we've been using for years to encrypt and protect data transferred over wireless networks on every device was no longer secure. A vulnerability called "KRACK" was uncovered, requiring every manufacturer to release a patch to protect against that vulnerability.

Some manufacturers did release a new firmware to deal with this vulnerability, but many did not, meaning you have to stop using the device or leave your network exposed.

In short, hardware devices, including home office routers, must be properly configured and, like everything, maintained regularly.

Layer # 3 – Antivirus Software

Antivirus software is the one layer that I find just about everywhere. Honestly, most companies have *something* in place.

In 2018 68 million pieces of new malware were released for the Windows platform alone. And, if you think your phone, tablet, or Macintosh computer isn't susceptible to malware and viruses, think again.

Unfortunately, it's no longer adequate to use free or even paid antivirus programs to protect against this constantly changing, rapidly growing threat.

We now recommend anti-malware software that people actively monitor. Since the malware program's first attempt to disable the antivirus software (giving the malware-free reign of your system), having monitored antivirus software adds a human layer of protection to software that often fails.

Layer # 4 – Web Content Filtering

Web content filtering may be provided by hardware or software and can be included as part of another piece of software such as your antivirus program or even as a component of email filtering software.

Web filtering works by reviewing each site you visit against a known malicious or phishing site database. The software maintains a database of such sites, much like antivirus software keeps a list of known malicious programs. For sites not in the database, the software reviews the page and, based on keywords, and overall content may block the site from being accessed.

This layer is crucial in today's environment and is the most overlooked.

Users can be directed to malicious websites by clicking links in phishing emails, mistyping a website's address, clicking on a search result, clicking on an ad on a page they are on, and from pop-ups. Additionally, they can be redirected to a website by malware already installed on the computer.

This layer of protection has an additional benefit to your business. A good content filtering program can be configured to block legitimate but unwanted sites during work hours.

For example, you may want to block timewasters such as Facebook for everyone in the office except the marketing staff. Or, you could block certain types of content, such as sites falling into the category of pornography or drug use. Another example would be to block sites that stream lots of content, such as music or video websites.

Besides protecting your network and data, the business implication of implementing filtering like this is improved productivity and increased bandwidth. Limiting where employees can go on the Internet leaves more bandwidth for business applications. Depending on your software and the Internet provider in your area, leveraging web filtering in this way can significantly increase the responsiveness of network applications.

Layer #5 - Email Filtering

More than ninety percent of targeted cyber attaches are reaching their victims through email right now. This means that protecting your inbox is one of the key layers in keeping your data and network safe.

Identity thieves and criminals carefully craft emails that appear legitimate or impersonate someone in your organization, looking to fool the recipient into disclosing sensitive information. This can be via an email conversation or by tricking the reader into clicking a link that directs them to a website to collect personal account information.

These emails are becoming more sophisticated, and they can even fool educated cybersecurity experts and trainers. Installing a layer of protection between the outside world and your inbox helps filter out these unwanted messages and has additional business benefits.

It's important to note that email filtering differs from relying on your email service or Outlook's junk or spam folder. While helpful in sorting out unwanted emails from the rest of your communications, the email has already been delivered to your inbox.

In contrast, an email filter receives and reviews all emails before they are delivered to your inbox. This prevents them from being opened accidentally (often enough to launch a virus or exploit a vulnerability) and from taking up space and resources on your internal network. This means more productivity as staff spends less time sorting through emails to find what's truly important, a lower burden on computing resources such as storage space, and lower costs and requirements related to system backups.

A good filtering system also provides you with additional control over your corporate data, such as the ability to globally blacklist and filter unwanted emails, archive emails, and provide failover if your primary email system fails.

Layer #6 - Backup and Disaster Recovery

Not too long-ago backup solutions were not considered a part of your security suite. However, that's no longer the case.

The advent of Ransomware has made this layer necessary. Ransomware is malicious software that quietly scrambles and encrypts your network files. It does this in the background without alerting anyone until it's too late. Once completed, the software notifies users of what has happened and demands a ransom be paid to decrypt the files. These ransoms have ranged from a couple of hundred dollars to millions in some high-profile cases.

After a ransomware attack, you have two options, pay the ransom and hope the criminal provides the key, or restore your systems from backup.

Unfortunately, most small businesses still have ineffective, old-school backups. Here's what one of those looks like. Is it you?

If your backup runs once a night and backs up files to a hard drive that someone in your staff is supposed to swap out every morning and take home with them, you are setting yourself up for failure.

You see, you may not realize that this type of backup is practically worthless today. Let me explain.

Without getting too technical here, if I needed to restore your server or critical computer to a functioning state from this type of backup due to a ransomware attack or because of a software or hardware failure, it would take me hours and possibly even a day or two (if I had to order a part). The process is long and painful, and costly. Plus, if your system fails on 4 pm Thursday, and your most recent backup was from 11 pm on Wednesday, you've lost a whole work-days worth of data that must be re-created. All the while, your business is down because of this process.

In today's business environment, this type of downtime and cost isn't acceptable. What you need to focus on truly is not backups but business continuity. How quickly and cost-effectively can your business be back up and running after some event, such as a hardware or software failure or a cyberattack?

The backup and disaster recovery solutions required in today's economy should meet the following criteria:

First, backups should occur several times throughout the day. This can be as frequently as hourly. This strategy alone can save your business hundreds, if not thousands of dollars. The more often you back up your data, the more you reduce your risk of failing the previous backup. Failed backups happen more than you imagine and, by having multiple opportunities throughout the day, as opposed to once per day, you increase your chances of having a good backup you can use when you need it.

Next, your backups should be snapshots, not just files. Each backup should be a complete image of the server or computer you are protecting. This significantly reduces the time it takes to get your business back up and running because we restore the entire system at once, not by rebuilding the computer and then restoring your data.

Third, your backup and disaster recovery system must be monitored and verified consistently. In my 30 years in this business, I've found that few people check to see that the backup worked; it still must be tested despite the software reports about a backup being successful. When it comes time to restore your data, you need to be certain that it's possible and no data corruption has occurred.

Having your backup off-site is the next priority. Leaving that hard drive in a drawer, or right next to the device you just backed up, or in your car, just isn't good enough. While rare, a fire, water pipe burst, or break-in that damages or destroys all those backup drives make them worthless. Instead, I recommend that your backups automatically be encrypted and sent offsite to a secure location. Additionally, this makes retrieving your data due to an event that prevents access to your business location less of an issue, allowing your company to be back up and running quickly.

Finally, the best scenario allows your backup solution, which is doing everything I mentioned above, to act as a replacement to your server. This means that either via a local backup device in your office or a remote location, the data has been backed up to, can be 'activated,' and a copy of your system is up and running and accessible in minutes, not hours.

In summary, old-school backup techniques aren't good enough to protect your data and business. You need something that provides frequent, tested, and automated data backup verified by people and has a feature allowing you to be back up and running in minutes instead of days or hours.

Fortunately, these types of backup and business continuity solutions are readily available and less costly than you might think, especially when compared to the expense and stress of losing your company's valuable data and the downtime a cyberattack or other event can cause.

Layer # 7 - Education

We've come to the final layer in our security model for your small business. The truth is that even if you properly implement all the layers up to this point, no solution is 100% secure. The bad guys are constantly working to circumvent each of these layers.

Identity thieves and cybercriminals have turned their attention to targeting us as individuals in very non-technical ways to access our data. Email and the phone are two powerful tools that criminals are using.

This means that it's now necessary to train your staff on the current threats to protect your company completely. Just as you might train employees about safe work habits and procedures, you must provide education on how to properly identify fake emails, websites, and other clever tricks that cybercriminals employ.

Ongoing education via webinars and in-person training is growing in availability. It provides a cost-effective way to get your staff familiar with keeping your company and clients' data safe.

Zero Trust for Your Small Business

Small businesses move quickly. They grow, add staff, and equipment at what often seems like a hectic pace, making cybersecurity exceptionally difficult, especially when staff often do not see the value. As a result, it is common for small businesses to fall victim to cybercriminals that always seem to be moving faster than they can deploy security measures.

Fortunately, with the zero trust approach to cybersecurity, even small companies may secure their systems and data, even in a rapid growth mode. Moreover, when viewed as an additional means of preventing ransomware, zero trust reduces the chance of a catastrophic data breach (Bocetta, 2020).

Here are some key zero trust security steps to use to avoid costly, time-consuming data breaches:

- All real-time account access, including metadata, should be tracked and monitored so that you have a complete picture of each user's intentions and activities. You should also be aware of who is entering your company's network. When it comes to cybersecurity, monitoring user activity is critical. It allows you to identify abuse as it occurs and take appropriate measures.

- If you have accounts with access to critical intellectual property or consumer information, protect them with strong passwords. A good password manager can help create long and complex passwords while generating new ones on your behalf, so they're never repeated!

- Require and verify that multifactor authentication is enabled everywhere and for every employee, contractor, partner, or administrator account. One of the essential security steps you can take is to employ multiple authentications. It significantly decreases the odds of a malicious agent obtaining access to the appropriate accounts.

- Restrict access to network devices as part of your zero trust path. Small firms are under continual time constraints. They frequently overlook fundamental security precautions in their rush to meet their various objectives. Thus, only allowing users restricted access from the beginning and promptly removing accounts as users leave are essential basic security steps.

- Never leave a default password. Any manufacturer-set passwords or sign in credentials, for example, must be updated immediately. Default passwords are simple to break and well-known to hostile actors. This simple, neglected step is frequently the source of data breaches and malware infestations.

- Verify that only those that absolutely actively need remote access to your network have it and are connecting securely. This includes deactivating remote access when it's not required and setting guidelines for connecting to your workplace remotely, requiring a VPN while connecting, or using personal hotspots instead of public wireless networks.

Zero trust can help you build a secure, flexible organization that can handle the most common causes of data breaches. The misuse of privileged access information is the most serious of these issues. These key elements of zero trust may assist any company in improving its management and IT management.

When you use the zero trust method, your security is always first, giving you visibility into where your data is and who has access to it.

What are the drawbacks or challenges, especially regarding small businesses (under 50 PCs) implementing zero trust?

The zero trust paradigm complicates security policy with these new security features for smaller businesses. Here are a few more problems that come with such a comprehensive strategy:

Time and effort set up. It might be challenging to rearrange policies inside an established network. If your network doesn't conform to zero trust architecture, you may need to set it up properly. This may require the assistance of IT Professionals and even a network overhaul. (O'Brien, 2021).

Comprehensive management for various users. Tracking all internal and external users and what they can access can be daunting. For example, you have to keep track of where data is stored and who has access to it. Ideally, the software monitors user accounts and behaviors, alerting IT staff of any unusual behavior. But this level of monitoring may not be feasible for smaller companies because of a lack of internal resources or the funds to outsource this type of service.

You are managing too many devices. According to some estimates, every employee now has five devices connected to the company's data. Furthermore, various devices may have distinct capabilities, making monitoring them difficult. Keeping track of the computers and mobile devices connected to your network and data is tough.

You have to monitor applications. Likewise, applications differ. Apps are often cloud-based and cross-platform. They are accessible to third parties. According to the zero trust philosophy, users of apps are organized, monitored, and adapted to their needs. Tracking how each application or vendor does this can become a chore.

Security across locations. Small businesses with multiple locations add additional complexity to the zero trust model. You must know where all your data is and how it's accessed, regardless of its physical location.

How does it work against ransomware?

A zero trust defense scheme may assist you in avoiding ransomware assaults. The notion "never trust, always" prevents malware from spreading throughout your entire system by blocking data access until the user or device authenticates as a trusted source. Furthermore, each new access request is reviewed again.

Here are four components in the zero trust model that businesses should use to protect against ransomware:

1. As much as feasible, create tiny network components and micro-perimeters to control traffic flow and user rights and access. For example, you may implement a public wireless network for vendors and guests totally separate from your internal wireless network. Segment your data into smaller,

protected components and limit access to that data to only those users and devices that need it.
2. Using comprehensive analytics and automation improves feedback and response. For example, monitoring and alerting software can provide real-time feedback on user applications, access rights, and who has what kind of access to data. These can alert you about odd behaviors to be investigated, such as someone accessing an employee's Microsoft 365 account from another country.
3. Security solutions need to be simple for users, vendors, and clients to be effective. Therefore, ensuring that the tools and techniques you implement are easy to use will go a long way to protecting your business. One example is single sign-on, an authentication method where companies allow their users to sign in to multiple accounts with a single account and password.
4. Whenever possible, include end-to-end encryption between all users, data, and devices. Combined with device and user monitoring, encryption provides added security against ransomware.

When small businesses try to implement a zero trust security model as part of their strategy to combat ransomware, they face several problems. Managing numerous devices and applications and data protection across locations are two examples of difficulties companies face. However, even modest organizations may overcome these hurdles by applying techniques such as gathering comprehensive analytics and automation, breaking down data into smaller, protected networks, using simple authentication techniques, and implementing end-to-end encryption.

Assembling Your Incidence Response Team

Knowing what to do when you have a breach is just as important as working to prevent one. The following sections have sample forms for you to use if you have a breach.

Depending on your company's size, your response team may be just you or have others on your team. Your incidence response team is the people that will oversee working through a potential data breach. Here's a sample form you can use to document and assemble your company's Incident Response Team.

Before, during, and after a breach, we recommend all organizations work with a reputable attorney with experience in the breach field. We can provide consultative support to organizations; however, any information provided should not constitute legal advice. We assume no liability in connection with these templates or consultations provided.

Assembling a breach response team is an integral part of breach preparation. The members of a breach response team should be identified, each bringing their own skills to the group. In the event of a breach, the team will work together to address the situations and take appropriate actions based on the circumstances. The individuals selected and identified below should be made aware and agree to accept the responsibilities of this position. The composition of this group may depend on the organization's size, so identify each position to the best of the organization's ability. (An alternative Breach Response Team template is available in Appendix A)

<u>Team Leader</u> – The team leader will be responsible for the oversight of the group as a whole. These responsibilities include but are not limited to; developing and overall coordination with the team, updating breach response procedures as necessary, and ensuring the team stays on track for a timely response.

Name:
Email:
Phone:_____

<u>Information Technology</u> – A representative from the Information Technology (IT) department should be selected to oversee the technical aspects associated with a breach. This includes but is not limited to; initial breach investigation, mitigation of ongoing harm, and implementation of new technologies that can prevent future occurrences.

Name:
Email:
Phone:_____

Human Resources/PR/Outreach – An individual should be identified to lead the efforts in the communication department. Breaches, depending on size, will often involve notification steps where affected individuals or appropriate government entities are informed of the incident and the remediation steps taken by the organization. This individual will be tasked with producing and sending notifications along with responding to questions or issues raised by affected individuals.

Name:
Email:
Phone:_____

Legal Counsel – A representative from a legal team is a strong recommendation for a breach response team. Ideally this should be someone knowledgeable and experienced in these situations who can provide guidance from a legal perspective surrounding the actions taken by the team.

Name:
Email:
Phone:_____

Outside Vendors – Any outside or third-party vendors who may play a role in assisting with a breach should be identified. This could be data forensics companies, law enforcement or data breach resolution companies. If the breach had occurred within a 3rd party system, a representative from that team could play an important role as well.

	Name	Phone Number	Emergency Phone Number	Email Address
Team Leader				
IT Leader				
HR/PR/Outreach				
Legal Counsel				
Additional 3rd party vendor				
Additional 3rd party vendor				
Additional 3rd party vendor				

Sample Security Incident Response

It's time to take cybersecurity seriously. You can't avoid the issue any longer - no matter how small your company is, you need a plan for responding if hacked or experience a data breach at some point in the future

That's where our Security Incident Response document comes into play!

I've included a template you can adapt to your business. Remember, it's not critical that yours be overly complex, just that you give it some thought and know what you're going to do when a breach occurs.

Once you create your Incident Response Plan, don't keep it a secret. Share it with your team, so they know how to respond to a breach.

For example, what do you say if someone gets a phishing email from the bad guys, appearing to be sent on your behalf? You need to be careful about the information you make public, especially since you need to assess the situation and get the authorities involved. You don't want to complicate that process in any way.

Purpose of Policy

The purpose of the policy is to develop the response to and reporting of security incidents, including the identification of and response to suspected or known security incidents, the mitigation of the harmful effects of known security incidents, to the extent possible, and the documentation of security incidents and their outcomes.

It should be noted that breach definitions, remediation steps and breach notification steps vary between various federal regulations such as the Health Insurance Portability and Accountability Act (HIPAA), The Gramm-Leach-Bliley Act (GLB Act or GLBA) and other federal regulations. In addition, most state regulated breach laws vary between individual states. In is highly recommended to consult with breach experts or legal counsel to determine The Company's responsibilities.

Definitions

Breach

Breach means the acquisition, access, use, or disclosure of personally identifiable information (PII) or sensitive company data such as email, employee information, confidential information, etc. which compromises the security or privacy of the PII or sensitive company data.

Unsecured PII

Unsecured PII means PII that is not rendered unusable, unreadable, or indecipherable to unauthorized individuals through the use of a technology or methodology such as encryption. The definition of unsecured PII varies between different federal and state regulations.

Reporting and Response

1. The Company will ensure that all incidents, threats, or violations that affect or may affect the privacy, confidentiality, integrity, or availability of PII and sensitive company data will be reported and responded to.

2. The Company shall have a Security Incident Response Team (SIRT) charged with the responsibility of identifying, evaluating and responding to security incidents. The Privacy Security Officer shall oversee the activities of the SIRT.

1. The SIRT will be responsible for investigating all known or suspected privacy and security incidents.

2. The SIRT will document a procedure for all employees to follow to report privacy and security incidents. See **Appendix A – Security Incident Response Log or the Security Incidents Module in the Security Portal.**

3. The Company will ensure that all employees receive training on how to identify and report security incidents.

4. All employees must follow the documented procedure to report security incidents. In addition, employees must report all known or suspected security incidents.

5. All employees must assist the SIRT with any security incident investigations.

Breach Determination

The Security Incident Response Team (SIRT) will investigate all reported and suspected security breaches. The SIRT will refer to federal or state regulations to help with breach determination. Breach determination varies between federal regulations such as HIPAA and GLBA. In addition, breach determination varies significantly between state regulations (for example, what may be considered a breach in one state may not be a breach in another state).

Breach Notification

If the SIRT determines that a breach of unsecured PII has occurred, breach notification of affected individuals may be required. The SIRT will refer to federal or state regulations to help with breach notification requirements. Breach notification requirements varies between federal regulations such as HIPAA and GLBA. In addition, breach notification requirements varies significantly between state regulations (for example, one state may have breach notification requirements that varies significantly from breach notification requirements in another state).

Key elements of a breach notification include:

1. **Date of discovery**

Usually, a breach will be treated as discovered as of the first day the breach is known or by exercising reasonable diligence would have been known.

2. **Timeliness of notification**

The Company will provide the required notifications without unreasonable delay after discovery of a breach. The amount of time The Company has to notify affected individuals varies between federal and state regulations.

3. **Content of notification**

If required, a notification will be provided to each individual affected by the discovered breach. The notification should include the following:
- A brief description of what happened, including the date of the breach and the date of the discovery of the breach, if known;
- A description of the types of unsecured PII that were involved in the breach (such as whether full name, social security number, date of birth, home address, account number or other types of information were involved);
- Any steps individuals should take to protect themselves from potential harm resulting from the breach;
- A brief description of what The Company is doing to investigate the breach, to mitigate harm to individuals, and to protect against any further breaches; and
- Contact procedures for individuals to ask questions or learn additional information, which should include a telephone number, an email address, Web site, or postal address.
- The notification should be written in plain language.

4. **Methods of notification**

The following methods are usually used to notify individuals affected by the discovered breach:

1. **Written notice**

Written notification by first-class mail to the individual at the last known address of the individual or, via email if the individual agrees to email notice. The notification may be provided in one or more mailings as information is available.

If the individual is deceased notifications are usually sent to next of kin or personal representative

2. **Substitute notice**

If contact information is out of date and written notification cannot be made, a substitute notification may be used.

- A substitute notification usually in the form of either a conspicuous posting on The Company's home page of its Web site, or conspicuous notice in major print or broadcast media in geographic areas where the individuals affected by the breach likely reside. The notice should include a contact phone number.

5. **Notification to media**

In addition to notifying individuals of a known breach, a notification to the media may be required as well.

6. Notification to federal or state regulatory agencies

The Company may need to report breaches of unsecured information to federal or state regulatory agencies.

7. Notification by Third Party Service Providers

Third Party Service Provider responsible for a breach of The Company's PII or sensitive company data should be required to notify The Company within a pre-determined reasonable timeframe. The timeframe should be defined in a Service Provider Agreement.

Third Party Service Provider breaches may result in The Company having to notify The Company's affected individuals (such as customers, employees, etc.).

Appendix A – Security Incident Response Log

Incident Identification Information	
Name:	
Phone:	
Email:	
Date/Time Detected:	
System / Application Affected:	
Incident Summary	
Type of Incident Detected: (Denial of Service, Malicious Code, Unauthorized Access, Unauthorized Use / Disclosure, Unplanned System Downtime, Other)	
Description of Incident:	
Names of Others Involved:	
Incident Notification	
How Was This Notified? (Security Office, IT Personnel, Human Resources, Other)	
Response Actions **Include Start and Stop times**	
Identification Measures (Incident Verified, Accessed, Options Evaluated):	
Containment Measures:	
Evidence Collected (Systems Logs, etc.):	

Sample Breach Response Letter

You can use the breach response letter below to notify clients and vendors of a data theft. Before, during or after an attack make sure you are working with reputable attorneys in this field who have experience helping organizations recover from breaches.

We offer consultative support but don't provide legal advice. Any information provided should not constitute legal advice, and we assume no liability in connection with these templates or consultations provided.

Dear (affected individual),

This letter is a notification that (organization name) has experienced a recent data security breach that may have affected your sensitive personal and/or sensitive information. (Provide details of the breach. This will include date of incident and discovery date, a brief description of the incident, and the potential categories of PII and Sensitive Data that may have been compromised).

Steps we are taking

We are working diligently to actively investigate this situation. (Describe who you are working with to investigate this incident [local, state or federal authorities, data forensics groups]). (Provide the steps that you the organization are taking to mitigate the harm to the individuals and protect their information against future breaches [this could include; training, updating policies, conducting a thorough risk analysis, etc.]).

(be prepared to potentially offer free credit monitoring services to the affected individuals if necessary)

Steps you should take

We recommend that you call any of these three phone numbers below to place a fraud alert on your credit file. A fraud alert will not allow an individual to open any new accounts unless you are notified first.

Experian   Equifax   TransUnion   Innovis

1-888-397-3742   1-888-766-0008   1-800-680-7289   1-800-540-2505

By placing a fraud alert with one of these agencies it will automatically inform the other two agencies. You will also have the ability to obtain a free copy of your credit report, which we encourage you to obtain and review for any potentially fraudulent material. Be sure to carefully inspect these reports, looking for items such as accounts you did not create, inquires you did not initiate and any inaccurate personal information.

We recommend that you continue to monitor your credit reports in the future for these inconsistencies. A security freeze can also be implemented on your account which does not allow any new accounts to be created or information to be shared with creditors without your authorization. For more information on a security freeze, you can contact a representative at any of the above agencies.

We sincerely apologize for the inconveniences relating to this situation. (Organization name) takes the protection of your sensitive information seriously. We want to assure you that we are taking all appropriate actions to mitigate future instances.

Please contact us if you have any questions or concerns.

Sincerely,

(Privacy or Security Officer's name) Contact information (toll free phone number)

What Should You Do If You Get Ransomed?

We see more and more that insurance companies are demanding that we assume you will get ransomware at some point and be prepared for that. Since you're reading this, the thought has probably crossed your mind more than once and probably makes your stomach churn at the very prospect of it happening to you and your company.

If you become the unfortunate victim of one of these threats, there are a few things you should do almost immediately.

Hopefully, you already have a relationship with an outsourced IT firm. If so, you'll want to contact them immediately. Even if you only suspect that you have been infected, I recommend that you reach out right away to begin stopping it from getting worse. It's always less costly to catch something like this early and quickly than to wait until later because of embarrassment or fear.

Your IT firm will likely ask you to do the following things immediately:

- Take a deep breath. While this may certainly be an awful and traumatic experience, try and remain calm.
- Disconnect your computers from the Internet immediately. This may be as simple as disconnecting your network cables or turning off your computers' wi-fi connections, or you may be instructed to disable your Internet immediately. This will help stop the infection from contacting the attackers and sending any additional information back to them.
- Do not turn off your computers. While this may be your first instinct, it can do more harm than good at this point.
- Suppose you can identify that the ransomware infects just a certain machine or server. You may be asked to disconnect that computer entirely from the rest of the network by disconnecting the network cables.
- Your IT Firm may be able to identify the strain of ransomware. Often hackers are using older versions that have known decryption keys. Do not, however, go surfing the Internet on your own!
- They will likely discuss a plan to recover your data from backups and what that might entail in your situation.

It may be possible that the malware has sent out some emails on your behalf. If you have a customer or client that asks about the incident, you mustn't divulge too much information at this time. While most states now have requirements to notify affected customers in a timely fashion, that does not mean you have to do it immediately!

If you get a call or someone contacts your office and inquiries about why you are down, or anything else, do NOT say any of the following

- We have been hacked!
- Let me transfer you to that person that sent the email.
- We do not know what is happening!
- You did not open the email attachment, did you?
- We know that we sent out an email with a virus.

Instead, you may simply want to have some verbiage pre-written that you can have your staff use. Your goal is to be calm and reassuring, but without disclosing any details. For example

"Thanks for bringing that to our attention. I understand your concern. At this time, we are investigating the incident. While I can't say anything else at this time, as soon as we are done with our investigation, we will know more."

A few additional resources
https://www.ftc.gov/tips-advice/business-center/guidance/data-breach-response-guide-business

https://nmcdn.io/e186d21f8c7946a19faed23c3da2f0da/556712d9bf0f4cb2a916cc810687d52b/files/risk-management-resources/practice-guides/Data_Breach_Toolkit.pdf

You should also reach out to your cyber insurance company if you have one. They will provide additional recommendations and even legal assistance in dealing with the issue. It's also important that you follow their process to assist with a claim.

The Cybersecurity and Infrastructure Security Agency (CISA) recommends you contact the following if you are a victim of ransomware

- Local federal law enforcement field office
- File a complaint with Internet Crime Complaint Center (IC3)
- Contact CyWatch 1-855-292-3937

- Report to CISA

The question also comes up about whether or not you pay the ransom. First, don't do this immediately. It may be illegal to pay the ransom if the US government sanctions the country or hacking group that perpetrated the attack. No kidding!

Of course, the best course of action is to do everything possible to avoid a breach in the first place. I'll be discussing this in more detail in upcoming chapters.

Pulling it All Together

None of the layers I've discussed here represent a significant cost or burden for small businesses. Each, if done correctly, can be put into place in some fashion by even the most frugal company.

However, this is not to say that you should not seek professional assistance in implementing each layer. As I've mentioned, properly selecting and implementing the right software and hardware at each level is best left to a trusted IT partner. Without proper implementation, the layers can be worthless.

It's also crucial to mention that each layer requires occasional maintenance and follow-up. Like so many things in today's IT environment that are different from years past, you simply cannot adopt a *set-it-and-forget-it* attitude. Therefore, it's crucial to partner with an IT company that understands these layers and can discuss and implement them with you.

Thank you for taking your time to read to this point of the book. That tells me a lot about how seriously you take protecting your business.

I'd love the opportunity to learn more about your business and your thoughts about this book. Further, I'd welcome the opportunity to discuss your Cybersecurity and IT needs and see if we would be a good fit.

Feel free to contact my office at:

Cyberstreams
(206) 388-3084
www.cyberstreams.com

Glossary

Advanced Persistent Threat (APT): A type of targeted attack. APTs are characterized by an attacker who has time and resources to plan an infiltration into a network.

Adware: Software that displays advertisements on your computer.

Anonymizing proxy: Allow the user to hide their web browsing activity. They are often used to bypass web security filters—e.g., to access blocked sites from a work computer.

Autorun worm: Malicious programs that take advantage of the Windows AutoRun feature. When the device on which they are stored is plugged into a computer, they run automatically.

Access Point (as in Wireless): A wireless access point (WAP) is a physical device or configured node on a local area network (LAN) that connects wirelessly capable devices and wired networks using a wireless standard such as Wi-Fi or Bluetooth (Devon 2020).

Backdoor Trojan: Allows someone to take control of a user's computer without their permission.

Business Email Compromise (BEC): A scam targeting people in companies where the email appears to come from a superior

Boot sector malware: Malware that spreads by modifying the program that enables your computer to start up.

Botnet: A collection of infected computers that a hacker remotely controls.

Browser hijacker: Programs that change the default homepage and search engine in your Internet browser without your permission

Brute force attack: An attack in which hackers try many possible keyword or password combinations to gain unauthorized access to a system or file.

Buffer overflow: Occurs when a program stores excess data by overwriting other parts of the computer's memory, causing errors or crashes.

Caller ID Spoofing: A process where the caller ID appears to be coming from a different number than it is or uses an identifier that is faked (Anastasia 2019).

Command and control center: A computer that controls a botnet (a network of compromised computers). Some botnets use distributed command and control systems, making them more resilient.

Cookie: Files placed on your computer that allow websites to remember details.

Cybersecurity: The status of being safe from unlawful or unauthorized use of electronic data or the steps taken to attain this.

Cyberespionage: Cyber espionage is a type of cybercrime in which a corporation or government body takes confidential, sensitive data or intellectual property to gain an advantage over a competitor.

Cybercrime: Cybercrime is a criminal act committed against someone who uses a computer, its systems, or its online or offline applications. When information technology is used to perpetrate or cover up a crime, this is known as cybercrime.

Cyberattack: An effort to disable computers, steal data, or utilize a penetrated computer system to launch more attacks is referred to as a cyberattack (Technology 2020).

Cyber resiliency: The capacity of systems that use or are enabled by cyber resources to predict, endure, recover from, and adapt to adverse situations, pressures, attacks, or breaches.

Cloud computing: Cloud security is a type of cyber security that focuses on keeping cloud computing systems safe. This involves ensuring the privacy and security of data across internet infrastructure, apps, and platforms.

Cloud: It's a word that refers to a worldwide network of servers, each with its function. The cloud is not a physical object but rather a massive network of distant servers connected worldwide and designed to function as a unified ecosystem.

Compromise: Unlawful exposure of information or a breach of a system's security policy resulting in the unauthorized planned or accidental disclosure, alteration, destruction, or loss of an item.

Credentials: The term "credentials" refers to the process of verifying one's identification or the methods used to verify one's identity. They might be part of a certificate or other authentication procedure that enables a user's identity to be verified in connection to a network address or other system ID.

Clickjacking: A technique that uses a common element to mislead users into clicking on an unwanted link or icon.

Data leakage: The unauthorized exposure of information. It can result in data theft or data loss.

Data loss: The result of the accidental misplacement of data rather than its deliberate theft.

Data theft: The deliberate theft of information rather than its accidental loss.

DDoS: This is an acronym for distributed denial of service, a type of cyberattack. This attack attempts to render a service, such as a website, inoperable by "flooding" it with malicious traffic or data from various sources (often botnets).

A Denial-of-Service attack (DOS): An attack that prevents users from accessing a computer or website.

Defense in Depth: Defense in detail refers to the employment of many layers of security measures within an information technology system.

DNS hijacking: The Domain Name System (DNS) is the Internet's phone book. It allows computers to translate website names, like www.google.com, into IP address numbers to communicate with each other.

Dark Web: The area of the Internet that can only be accessed with specific software, letting users and website owners remain anonymous or untraceable.

Document malware: Malware that utilizes vulnerabilities in applications that let you read or edit documents.

Drive-by download: The infection of a computer with malware when a user visits a malicious website.

Exploit: An exploit takes advantage of a vulnerability to access or infect a computer.

Encryption in transit: When encrypted data is in transit, it's traveling between devices and networks like the internet, within an organization, or being transferred to the cloud.

Email headers: An email header is an area above the email content section to insert vital information. The receiver, the sender, and a subject line are all included in the header and the option of sending copies to other recipients.

Encryption: The process of turning data or information into a code, particularly to restrict unwanted access.

Encryption at rest: "Encryption at rest" implies that the data a program saves on its local storage is encrypted, preventing it from being read by an attacker who has access to the storage but not to the application.

Firewall: A firewall is a network security device that monitors incoming and outgoing network traffic and allows or denies data packets according to a set of security rules.

Fake antivirus malware: Reports non-existent threats to scare users into installing malicious software and paying for unnecessary product registration and cleanup.

Hacker: A hacker is any skilled computer expert who uses technical knowledge to overcome a problem or access a computer system.

Hacking: Gaining unauthorized access to data in a system or computer.

Hacktivism: The hacking activity is typically for political and social purposes, attacking corporations, governments, organizations, and individuals.

Hoax: Reports of false and unsubstantiated claims in an attempt to trick or defraud users.

Honey pot: A honeypot is a network-attached server put up as a ruse to attract cybercriminals and identify, block, or investigate a hacking way to gain illegal access to information systems. A form of trap security specialists uses to detect hacking attacks or collect malware samples.

Internet worm: Malware that replicates across the Internet or local networks.

Keylogging: The process of secretly recording keystrokes by an unauthorized third party.

Malware: A general term for malicious software. Malware includes viruses, worms, Trojans, and spyware. Many people use the terms malware and virus interchangeably.

Mobile phone malware: Malware intended to run on mobile devices, such as smartphones.

Malvertising: Incorporating malware into web commercials.

Multi-factor Authentication MFA: MFA is an authentication mechanism that requires a user to give two or more verification factors to access a resource such as an application, an online account, or a VPN.

Patches: A patch is a software update that consists of code that is placed (or patched) into the executable program's code. A patch is often applied to an existing software package. Patches are frequently used to address issues between complete versions of a software program.

Parasitic viruses: Also known as file viruses, spread by attaching themselves to programs.

Phishing emails: The process of deceiving recipients into sharing sensitive information with an unknown third party (cybercriminal).

Potentially unwanted application (PUA): Programs that are not malicious but may be unsuitable for use in a business environment and create security concerns.

Ransomware: Software that denies you access to your files or computer until you pay a ransom.

Rootkit: A piece of software that hides programs or processes running on a computer.

Router: A router is a piece of hardware that connects two or more packet-switched networks or subnetworks. It lets numerous devices connect to the Internet at the same time.

Social engineering: The methods attackers use to deceive victims into acting. Typically, these actions open a malicious web page or run an unwanted file attachment, or divulge confidential information.

Social networking: Websites allowing you to communicate and share information. But they can also be used to spread malware and steal personal information.

Spam: Spam is unsolicited bulk email, the electronic equivalent of junk mail, that comes to your inbox.

Spear phishing: Targeted phishing using spoof emails to persuade people within an organization to reveal sensitive information or credentials.

Spoofing (Email): When the sender address of an email is forged for social engineering purposes (Morgan 2020).

Spyware: Software that permits advertisers or hackers to gather sensitive information without your permission.

SQL injection: SQL injection exploits database query software that doesn't thoroughly test for correct queries.

Suspicious files and behavior: When an endpoint security solution scans files, it labels them as clean or malicious. If a file exhibits any suspicious characteristics or behavior, it is labeled suspicious.

Two-factor authentication 2FA: Two-factor authentication (2FA), often known as two-step verification or dual-factor authentication, is a security method in which users validate their identity using two independent authentication factors.

Threat Actor: Also called a malicious actor, is an entity that is partially or wholly responsible for a security incident that impacts – or has the potential to impact – an organization's security."

Trojan (Trojan horse): Malicious programs that pretend to be a legitimate software but carry out hidden, harmful functions.

Virus: Malicious computer programs that can spread to other files.

Vulnerability: Bugs or flaws in software programs that hackers exploit to compromise computers.

Zombie: An infected computer that a hacker remotely controls. It is part of a large group of compromised computers called a botnet.

Zero Trust: Zero trust is a security concept based on restrictive access limitations and not trusting anybody by default, including those already inside the network perimeter.

Resources

Anastasia. "45 Main Cyber Security Terms Everyone Must Know" 01 Nov. 2019 Web 01 Nov. 2019. https://spinbackup.com/blog/45-main-cybersecurity-terms-everyone-must-know/

Bocetta, S. How a small business can achieve Zero Trust security. Web 02 Mar. 2020 https://cybersecurity.att.com/blogs/security-essentials/how-a-small-business-can-achieve-zero-trust-security

Booth, Kathleen. "What Is CMMC? A Primer for Defense Industrial Base (DIB) Contractors." December 10, 2021. https://www.attilasec.com/blog/what-is-cmmc-dib-contractors.

Calvello, M. "A Complete Glossary:" 70+ Cyber Security Terms (A to Z) 17 Web Jun. 2019 https://www.g2.com/articles/cyber-security-terms

Carpenter, Perry, The Importance of A Strong Security Culture And How to Build One. Web 27 May 2021 https://www.forbes.com/sites/forbesbusinesscouncil/2021/05/27/the-importance-of-a-strong-security-culture-and-how-to-build-one/?sh=381172f86d49

Childress, Abigail Stokes, and Marcus. "CMMC Explained: What Defense Contractors Need to Know." CSO Online. CSO, April 8, 2020. https://www.csoonline.com/article/3535797/the-cybersecurity-maturity-model-certification-explained-what-defense-contractors-need-to-know.html

Crane, C. 15 Small Business Cybersecurity Statistics That You Need to Know. Web 09 Dec. 2020 https://www.thesslstore.com/blog/15-small-business-cyber-security-statistics-that-you-need-to-know/

Cybersecurity 101: Intro to the Top 10 Common Types of Cybersecurity Attacks. Web 17 Oct. 2021 https://www.infocyte.com/blog/2019/05/01/cybersecurity-101-intro-to-the-top-10-common-types-of-cyber-security-attacks/

Devon, 25 Cyber Security Terms That Everyone Who Uses A Computer Should Know. Web 23 Jul. 2020 https://www.cybintsolutions.com/20-cyber-security-terms-that-you-should-know/

Ijaz, Rehan, Ransomware: The Terrifying Overlooked Threat To Small Businesses in 2021. Web 19 Mar. 2021 https://www.smallbizdaily.com/ransomware-terrifying-overlooked-threat-small-businesses-in-2021/

Freitas, Roseann, "Ransomware Attacks Are Rising. Here's a Plan for…? Web 09 Jul. 2021 https://www.trust-bbb.org/torchtalk/ransomware-attacks-are-rising

Kath, Heath, Ransomware Attacks on Small Businesses: How to Mitigate. Web 21 Jul. 2021 https://www.goanywhere.com/blog/ransomware-attacks-on-small-businesses-how-to-mitigate

Kelley, Diana, "From Linear To ORBITAL: Rethinking Defense in Depth." Security Intelligence. 07 Mar. 2017 Web 26 Sept. 2021. https://securityintelligence.com/from-linear-to-orbital-rethinking-defense-in-depth/

Kessem, Limor, Data Breach Costs at Record High, Zero Trust, AI, and Automation Help Reduce Costs. Web 28 Jul. 2021 https://www.corporatecomplianceinsights.com/zero-trust-principles-for-cybersecurity/

Legislature, Washington State, Personal Information-Notice of security breaches. https://apps.leg.wa.gov/RCW/default.aspx?cite=19.255.010

Lenovo StoryHub, "Why Defense-in-depth Is Key to Defeating Ransomware." Web 14 Sept. 2021 https://news.lenovo.com/why-defense-in-depth-is-key-to-defeating-ransomware/

Limited, Cyberteam Security Services. "Defense in Depth Security Model. "Design and Coding by Datadean Limited. https://cyberteamsecurity.com/defence-depth-security-model.html

Marsden, Eric., "The Defense in Depth Principle a Layered Approach to Safety Barriers." Risk Engineering. Web 27 Aug. 2018 https://risk-engineering.org/concept/defence-in-depth

Martin, Scott, Why Your Business Needs to Adopt Zero Trust, and Automation Help Reduce Costs. Web 19 Jul. 2021 https://www.corporatecomplianceinsights.com/zero-trust-principles-for-cybersecurity/

Morgan, Steve, The Motherlist Glossary of Cybersecurity And Cybercrime Definitions. Web 02 Jan. 2020 https://www.corporatecomplianceinsights.com/zero-trust-principles-for-cybersecurity/

Midler, Marisa, "3 Ransomware Defense Strategies." SEI Blog. Web 09 Nov. 2020 https://insights.sei.cmu.edu/blog/3-ransomware-defense-strategies/

Networks, A.W., Basic Cybersecurity Terminology You Need to Know. Web 26 Feb 2021 https://arcticwolf.com/resources/blog/cybersecurity-101-basic-terminology-you-need-to-know

O'Brien, Mary, Zero Trust: Confidently Secure Your Business to Grow Fearlessly. 05 May 2021 https://securityintelligence.com/posts/confidently-secure-business-grow-fearlessly-zero-trust/

Pavithran, Apu. How To Implement A Zero Trust Model Of Cybersecurity Into Your Organization. 15 Jul. 2021 https://www.forbes.com/sites/forbestechcouncil/2021/07/15/how-to-implement-a-zero-trust-model-of-cybersecurity-into-your-organization/?sh=35e7f116680d

RCW 19.255.010: Personal information-notice of security breaches. (n.d.). Retrieved December 6, 2021, from https://apps.leg.wa.gov/rcw/default.aspx?cite=19.255.010.

Rosenbaum, Eric, Main Street overconfidence: America's small businesses aren't worried about hacking. Web 10 Aug. 2021 https://www.cnbc.com/2021/08/10/main-street-overconfidence-small-businesses-dont-worry-about-hacking.html

Shilling, Conor, The rising threat of cyberattacks – how can small businesses prepare? Web 09 Sep. 2021 https://www.simplybusiness.co.uk/knowledge/articles/2021/09/cyber-attacks-on-small-businesses/

Steinberg, Scott, Cyberattacks now cost companies $200,000 on average, putting many out of business. Web 13 Oct. 2019 https://www.cnbc.com/2019/10/13/cyberattacks-cost-small-companies-200k-putting-many-out-of-business.html

Technology, Smart Eye, 12 Common Cybersecurity Terms. Web 06 Oct. 2020 https://blog.smarteyetechnology.com/12-most-common-cyber-security-words

Tharnish, Shena, Cyberattacks Become More Prevalent, Here's Why Your Small Business is at Risk. Web 28 Feb. 2020 https://www.securitymagazine.com/articles/91806-as-cyber-attacks-become-more-prevalent-heres-why-your-small-business-is-at-risk

Thomas, Steve, How to build a culture of security. Web 20 Nov. 2020 https://www.securitymagazine.com/articles/93980-how-to-build-a-culture-of-security

Tung, Liam, Zero trust and cybersecurity: Here's what it means and why it matters. Web 06 Sep. 2021 https://www.zdnet.com/google-amp/article/zero-trust-and-cybersecurity-heres-what-it-means-and-why-it-matters/

Weaver, Aaron, Here's the Single Largest Cybersecurity Threats To Small Businesses. Web 20 Apr. 2021 https://hacked.com/cybersecurity-threat-to-small-businesses/

Witts, Joel, The Top 5 Biggest Cybersecurity Threats That Small Businesses Face And How To Stop Them. Web 20 Jul. 2021 https://expertinsights.com/insights/the-top-5-biggest-cyber-security-threats-that-small-businesses-face-and-how-to-stop-them/

YEC, How To Protect Your Small Business From Cyber Threats. 02 Jun. 2021 https://www.forbes.com/sites/theyec/2021/06/02/how-to-protect-your-small-business-from-cyber-threats/?sh=5702b08f56cd

www.ingramcontent.com/pod-product-compliance
Lightning Source LLC
Chambersburg PA
CBHW021441210526
45463CB00002B/603